RESTORING THE UNITY IN FAITH
THE ORTHODOX–ORIENTAL ORTHODOX THEOLOGICAL DIALOGUE

D1559997

RESTORING THE UNITY IN FAITH

THE ORTHODOX–ORIENTAL ORTHODOX
THEOLOGICAL DIALOGUE

An Introduction with Texts

Edited by
Thomas FitzGerald
Emmanuel Gratsias

The Joint Commission of Eastern and Oriental Orthodox Churches

The Standing Conference of
Canonical Orthodox Bishops
in the Americas

The Standing Conference of
Oriental Orthodox Churches
of America

Holy Cross Orthodox Press
Brookline, Massachusetts

© 2007 by
The Joint Commission of Eastern and Oriental Orthodox Churches

Published by
Holy Cross Orthodox Press
50 Goddard Avenue
Brookline, Massachusetts 02445

ISBN-13: 978-1-885652-93-5
ISBN-10: 1-885652-93-3

Library of Congress Cataloging-in-Publication Data

Restoring the unity in faith : the Orthodox-Oriental Orthodox theologi-
cal dialogue : an introduction with texts / edited by Thomas FitzGerald,
Emmanuel Gratsias.
p. cm.
"The Joint Commission of Eastern and Oriental Orthodox Churches, the
Standing Conference of Canonical Orthodox Bishops in the Americas, the
Standing Conference of Oriental Orthodox Churches of America."
ISBN-13: 978-1-885652-93-5
ISBN-10: 1-885652-93-3
1. Orthodox Eastern Church--Relations--Oriental Orthodox Churches.
2. Oriental Orthodox churches--Relations--Orthodox Eastern Church.
3. Ecumenical movement--Orthodox Eastern Church. 4. Ecumeni-
cal movement--Oriental Orthodox churches. I. FitzGerald, Thomas E.,
1947- II. Gratsias, Emmanuel, 1941- III. Joint Commission of Eastern and
Oriental Orthodox Churches. IV. Standing Conference of Canonical Orthodox Bishops in America. V. Standing Conference of Oriental Orthodox
Churches.
BX324.45.R47 2007
281'.5--dc22
                                                                    2008002653

In loving remembrance

Fr. Emmanuel J. Gratsias
1941–2007

Founding member

The Joint Commission of
Eastern and Oriental Orthodox Churches

May his memory be eternal

CONTENTS

STANDING CONFERENCE OF THE CANONICAL ORTHODOX BISHOPS IN THE AMERICAS

February 28, 2006

Dearly Beloved,

This volume has been prepared by the Joint Commission of Oriental and Eastern Orthodox Churches. This commission was established in 2000 by the Standing Conference of Canonical Orthodox Bishops in the Americas and the Standing Conference of Oriental Orthodox Churches.

This volume is intended to help you and your faithful understand what has already transpired in the efforts to restore the unity in Faith that was disrupted in the fifth century. In it, therefore, you will find for your edification Statements from Theological Consultations and those of the official Joint Theological Commission, together with an introductory analytical paper on *The Orthodox-Oriental Orthodox Theological Dialogue*.

On this North American continent, where we all live together and have daily and increasing contact with one another, the sense of urgency is perhaps more pronounced than in other parts of the world. Closer contact and cooperation among Eastern Orthodox and Oriental Orthodox parishes and faithful in North America will help dispel stereotypes and false information, and will promote friendship and understanding.

May our Lord, Jesus Christ, bless this noble endeavor.

†Archbishop DEMETRIOS
Chairman, Standing Conference
of the Canonical Orthodox Bishops in the Americas

THE STANDING CONFERENCE OF
ORIENTAL ORTHODOX CHURCHES *of* AMERICA

I T GIVES ME GREAT PLEASURE to see the publication of this volume on *The Orthodox-Oriental Orthodox Theological Dialogue*, sponsored by the Standing Conference of Canonical Orthodox Bishops in the Americas, and the Standing Conference of Oriental Orthodox Churches of America. On behalf of the latter group, I convey our congratulations and blessings to all involved in realizing this project.

As offspring of the "Orthodox World," our respective churches share many things in common, chief among them a long memory—a long *experience*—of history. We have lived through many seasons, and have witnessed many purposes under heaven. We have known golden ages of artistic flowering; we have suffered under dark days of tyranny and death. Many of us alive today are products of the violent dispersion of our people in the past. Yet we remain representatives of *living* nations and *vital* Christian traditions—alive, building, and looking with optimism to the future.

We Orthodox have our roots in the great cultures of deep antiquity. At decisive moments each of us placed our national destinies into the hands of the Biblical God. We have exalted the great, humane sentiments resident in the Christian religion, and have produced great figures who embodied those sentiments. We know the face of virtue, just as we recognize the face of wickedness. We are a thread of continuity, linking the great civilizations of the past with the great civilization of the present. Great wisdom resides in that vast experience, which would surely be a valuable contribution to the civilized world at large, as it considers the great issues of our own time.

For that reason, among others, this volume outlining the long and fruitful dialogue between our two Orthodox "families" is timely and most welcome. We hope and pray that it will contribute to an atmosphere of deeper friendship and solidarity among our churches and their respective flocks.

With prayers,

Abp. K. Barsamian

Archbishop Khajag Barsamian
Chairman, Standing Conference of Oriental Orthodox Churches of America

July 13, 2006

Restoring the Unity in Faith: The Orthodox–Oriental Orthodox Theological Dialogue

Thomas FitzGerald[1]

The Orthodox Church and the Oriental Orthodox churches throughout the world are engaged in a process of reconciliation. This process is aimed at affirming the same faith and restoring full communion between the two families of churches. This process is taking place through theological dialogue, common witness and service, and prayer. The division between the Orthodox Church and the Oriental Orthodox churches dates from the period following the Council of Chalcedon in the year AD 451.

The holy synods of all the autocephalous Orthodox churches and the autocephalous Oriental Orthodox churches have formally blessed and encouraged this process of reconciliation. The

[1] Thomas FitzGerald, protopresbyter of the Ecumenical Patriarchate–Greek Orthodox Archdiocese of America, is Dean and Professor of Church History and Historical Theology at Holy Cross Greek Orthodox School of Theology.

Portions of this essay first appeared as "Towards the Reestablishment of Full Communion: The Orthodox–Oriental Orthodox Dialogue," *Greek Orthodox Theological Review* 36:2 (1991), 169–88.

churches have affirmed that their divisions from each other are contrary to the reconciling message of the gospel of Christ. Our Lord has prayed that his followers be united in a manner that reflects the unity of the persons of the Holy Trinity (John 17). The churches have also affirmed that their divisions inhibit their witness to Christ in the world today.

Informal theological dialogues between theologians from both families of churches began in 1964. These dialogues benefited from renewed studies of the theological and historical issues of the fifth and sixth centuries. These dialogues and the related studies also provided the churches with new perspectives on the old issues of division.

Because of these theological studies and preliminary dialogues, the Orthodox Church and the Oriental Orthodox churches formally acted to establish a commission for theological dialogue. This was a clear expression of the desire of the churches to address the issues of division. The Joint Commission for Theological Dialogue between the Orthodox Church and the Oriental Orthodox churches first met in 1985. Since then, it has produced official statements in 1989 and 1990. These statements were reaffirmed at a meeting of the Plenary Commission in 1993. The commission has also encouraged greater understanding and cooperation between the two families of churches at the regional and local levels.

The results of the formal theological dialogue have been remarkable. Through their studies, the official representatives of the churches have examined all aspects of the division. In its statements, the commission has concluded that both the Orthodox and the Oriental Orthodox share the same historic apostolic faith despite over fifteen centuries of formal separation. The Joint Commission has recommended that the churches take the appropriate steps to end their division and to restore their unity.

The churches are now studying the agreed-upon statements of these formal theological dialogues and their practical recommendations. The ultimate goal of the theological dialogue is the restoration of full communion through the profession of the apostolic faith. This unity in faith will be expressed in the sharing of the Holy Eucharist.

The unity of the churches means a true communion of churches that profess the same apostolic faith and are united in the teaching of that faith. Unity in faith does not mean the absorption of one church by another. The unity in the faith recognizes a diversity of customs and traditions that are part of the life of the churches. Unity does not mean uniformity in all aspects of church life. Rather, unity in the historic Orthodox faith can also treasure the distinctive history, liturgical traditions and cultural inheritance of the various churches. This diversity, however, should not impede unity in the faith and the communion of the churches.

Here in North America, the relationship between the Orthodox and Oriental Orthodox has been developing both informally and formally for more than fifty years. Already there have been many valuable opportunities for cooperation in the areas of theological education, youth ministry, and religious education. There have also been valuable opportunities for cooperation in the areas of ministerial and priestly formation. Some local parishes have also already developed opportunities for cooperation.

Recognizing the advances made here and in other parts of the world, the Standing Conference of Canonical Orthodox Bishops and the Standing Conference of Oriental Orthodox Churches established in the United States a joint commission in 2000. The commission seeks to assist in the process of restoring unity. The activities of this commission will build upon the theological agreements that the churches have achieved already. The commission is especially concerned with increasing contacts and cooperation among the bishops, clergy, and laity of the two families of churches. Since the year 2001, the commission has sponsored an annual service of prayer in the New York City area.

Historical and Theological Background

The Church and the Apostolic Faith

The life of the Church is centered upon Jesus Christ and his gospel. Christ is our Lord and Savior. As the Word of God, the Lord took flesh and dwelt among us for our salvation (John 1:1–18). He united himself with us in order to restore us to communion with God the Father through the Holy Spirit. As the "light of the world" (John 8:12), Christ revealed to us the depth of divine love for us. In so doing, the Lord taught us about the triune God: the Father, Son, and Holy Spirit. He affirmed the dignity of the human person created in the "image and likeness" of God. Our Lord taught us that we are created to live in communion with God and with one another in the midst of creation. As "the way, the truth, and the life" (John 14:6), Christ revealed to us a new way of living. He taught us to "love the Lord your God with all your heart, with all your soul, and with all your strength, and with all your mind; and your neighbor as yourself" (Luke 10:27). He established the Church as a community of believers who honor God in worship and proclaim the message of the gospel. As the risen Lord, Jesus conquered the power of sin, Satan, and death. Today, the Lord is not a remote figure of the past. He is present in our midst. He promised to be with us always!

From the time of Pentecost, the apostles and disciples were obedient to the command of the Lord to preach the gospel throughout the whole world (Matt 28:18–20). The Church was truly a missionary community of faith. The message of Christ was not meant to be confined to a particular place or to a particular people. Wherever the early missionaries went, they preached the gospel and Christian communities were established. This pattern has been followed through the centuries. From the very beginning, the Church that Jesus established guided believers in their relationship with the triune God and with one another. The Church is a sign and an expression of the salutary relationship that God offered to all.

Because of her concern for the salvation of all, the Church has always sought to teach and to preserve the faith free from distortion. The Church has opposed false teachings, which challenge the essential and saving truths of the gospel. In using limited human language to describe the mighty acts of the loving God, the Church has expressed her faith in a way that both forms its members and maintains its members' unity. Ultimately, this concern for teaching the faith and preserving the unity of the Church was rooted in its faithfulness to the Lord and was expressed in its desire to guide all towards salvation. As the community of faithful believers, the Church has been the sacred instrument of the triune God who "desires that all be saved and come to a knowledge of the truth" (1 Tim 2:4).

The Councils of Nicaea and Constantinople

The early encounter with peoples and cultures beyond Palestine also raised new challenges for the Church. Among the most serious doctrinal challenges were questions related to the understanding of the Holy Trinity. During the first four centuries of its life, the Church was challenged to express its faith and to defend it against distortions and heresies. Among the early heresies were the teachings of Arianism, Gnosticism, and Pneumatomachianism. Each of these heresies presented distorted views of the persons of the Holy Trinity, often with misleading references to the Scriptures and Tradition.

The early fathers and mothers of the Church responded to these heresies. They sought to defend the faith and maintain unity among Christ's followers. The great teachers always explicated the apostolic faith in relationship to questions being raised through a proper interpretation of Scripture and the early Tradition. When necessary, they also acted to restore the unity of believers wherever possible through a common profession of faith.

The Council of Nicaea in 325 and the Council of Constantinople in 381 were important meetings of bishops at which the faith of the Church was expressed in opposition to a number of heresies including Arianism, which denied the full divinity of Christ. In their creedal affirmations, the councils did not create the apostolic faith. Rather, the councils bore witness to the apostolic faith in relationship to the distorted teachings of the time.

The Nicene–Constantinopolitan Creed, which emerged from these councils, became an important expression of the apostolic faith. Since that time, this creed has been used in preaching and teaching the faith by all the Orthodox and Oriental Orthodox churches. The creed has also been used as an expression of unity among the churches and as a basis for restoring unity among divided believers.

The Council of Ephesus

During the early fifth century, the Church was confronted with new challenges related to its understanding of the person of Christ. Affirming the experience of the first Christians, the Church always taught that Christ was both truly and fully divine, as well as truly and fully human. This was an affirmation of the mystery of the incarnation of the Son of God. By the early fifth century, however, new questions began to be raised about the relationship of divinity and humanity in Christ as well as about the appropriate terminology to express this reality.

Especially significant were the different perspectives on Christology, which characterized the theological traditions of Alexandria and Antioch in that period. The Alexandrian tradition emphasized the unity of humanity and divinity in Christ. The Antiochian tradition emphasized the distinctiveness of humanity and divinity in Christ. Both traditions in their best expressions affirmed that Christ is fully human and fully divine. However, both traditions looked at the reality of Christ from different perspectives. Moreover, both traditions often used the same theological terms differently. Both perspectives on the mystery of Christ were correct and complementary, provided they were not pushed to an extreme.

This is precisely what happened with the Nestorian heresy

in the fifth century. Nestorius and his followers emphasized the distinctiveness and integrity of humanity and divinity in Christ to such a degree that they could not easily affirm a true unity of the two in the single person of Christ. The sign of this difficulty was the unwillingness of Nestorius to refer to Mary as the Theotokos. The perspectives of Nestorius and his followers pushed the Antiochian perspective to an extreme.

Opposed by St. Cyril of Alexandria, the position of Nestorius and likeminded teachers was formally rejected at the Council of Ephesus in 431. At this council, the christological teachings of St. Cyril were affirmed. At that time, the Cyrilian statement that that the incarnate Word was one nature (*physis*) became the hallmark of the opposition to Nestorianism. In this instance, St. Cyril was using the phrase "one nature" (*physis*) to mean "one person." Sadly, the initial actions of this council led to a break in the relationship between the Patriarchate of Alexandria and the Patriarchate of Antioch.

Fortunately, moderate teachers in both churches repudiated the division and actively sought to heal it. By the year 433, the differences between the two churches were resolved under the leadership of Patriarch Cyril of Alexandria and Patriarch John of Antioch. An historic statement of reconciliation and unity was agreed upon. This statement spoke of Christ as one person of two natures and clearly opposed the extreme teaching of Eutyches. At the same time, it sought to clarify terminology. In accepting the two-nature terminology in 433, St. Cyril recognized that the phrase "two natures" could also be used in reference to the divine and human realities in the one Christ. This agreement ultimately led many in the Church of Antioch to accept the decision of the Council of Ephesus.

In the course of time, however, some elements of the Church in East Syria and the Persian Empire refused to accept the Council of Ephesus and the agreement of 433. This eventually led to the development of the Assyrian Church of the East, at that time located chiefly in the region of the Persian Empire. It is worth noting that St. Isaac the Syrian of Niniva, the great teacher in the late seventh century, was a member of this church. Yet both the Orthodox and the Oriental Orthodox honor him as a saint.

There also was an extreme reaction to the position of Nestorius and similar teachers led by the Alexandrian monk Eutyches and his followers. They emphasized the unity of the divine and human in Christ in such a way that his full humanity was not preserved in the union. It appeared as though the humanity was lost through its contact with the divine. The teachings of Eutyches pushed the Alexandrian tradition to an extreme.

The Eutychians were true "dogmatic Monophysites" because they taught that Christ's human nature was subsumed by his divine nature. In speaking of the "one nature" of Christ, the followers of Eutyches did not properly affirm the integrity of the divine and human in the one Christ. However, their extreme views dominated another meeting of bishops held in Ephesus in 449 under the leadership of Patriarch Dioscorus of Alexandria. Although this meeting was subsequently repudiated, it created a true crisis that divided a number of the regional churches.

The Council of Chalcedon

A new council of bishops was held in the city of Chalcedon, near Constantinople, in 451. It was designed to heal the growing christological division. This council was a bold and swift reaction to the meeting of bishops held in Ephesus in 449. That gathering, dubbed the "Robber Synod" by Pope Leo of Rome, had expressed an extreme Alexandrian Christology. The bishops at Chalcedon repudiated the council of 449 and deposed Patriarch Dioscorus of Alexandria because of his role in that gathering.

The bishops at Chalcedon were concerned with bearing witness to the fullness of the apostolic faith in opposition to extremes in both the Alexandrian and the Antiochian traditions. The council was also concerned with reconciling the ever-widening division between the regional churches, which were expressing divergent theological tendencies especially in the wake of the council of 449. Although they were opposed to the extreme tendencies of Eutyches, the bishops affirmed the christological teachings expressed by St. Cyril of Alexandria.

The bishops of the Council of Chalcedon did not wish to create a new creed. Indeed, the Council of Ephesus had forbidden the creation of a new creed that would supplant the Creed of Nicaea of 325. Yet the bishops clearly wished to reject both the heresy of Nestorianism and the heresy of Eutychianism. In rejecting the decision of the council of 449 and the extreme tendencies reflected in it, the bishops recognized the need to fashion a statement of faith that would express more clearly the Church's understanding of reality of Christ.

They also recognized the need to come to an agreement on theological terms. Theological differences had been compounded by the fact that key words such as *physis* (nature), *hypostasis* (nature/substance), *ousia* (substance), and *prosopon* (person) were often used differently in different contexts. There was not full agreement as to how the terms should be used with reference to the reality of Christ. The statement of Chalcedon, therefore, must be understood within the context of the christological differences reaching back before the Council of Ephesus in 431 and the differing theological terms being used to describe Christ.

The statement of the Council of Chalcedon affirmed that Christ is one person in whom there is a human nature and a divine nature. Each nature is full and complete. Neither his divine nor his human nature is diminished or lost by the union in one person. The two natures exist in Christ "without confusion, without change, without division, and without separation." The statement of the council further affirmed that "the difference between the natures is in no way removed because of the union, but rather the peculiar property of each nature is preserved and both combine in one person and in one hypostasis." While recognizing the profound mystery of the incarnation of the Son of God, the statement affirmed that Christ is one person in two natures.

This statement of Chalcedon opposed both the extreme position of the Alexandrians represented by Eutyches and the extreme position of the Antiochians represented by followers of Nestorius. At the same time, the statement of Chalcedon sought to be faithful to the teachings of St. Cyril of Alexandria.

The statement of Chalcedon says in part:

> Therefore, following the holy fathers, we all with one accord teach men to acknowledge one and the same Son, our Lord Jesus Christ, at once complete in Godhead and complete in manhood, truly God and truly man, consisting also of a reasonable soul and body; of one substance with the Father as regards his Godhead, and at the same time of one substance with us as regards his manhood; like us in all respects, apart from sin; as regards his Godhead, begotten of the Father before the ages, but yet as regards his humanity begotten, for us humans and for our salvation, of Mary the Virgin, the God-bearer; one and the same Christ, Son, Lord, Only-begotten, recognized in two natures, without confusion, without change, without division, without separation; the distinction of natures being in no way annulled by the union, but rather the characteristics of each nature being preserved and coming together to form one person and subsistence, not as parted or separated into two persons, but one and the same Son and Only-begotten God the Word, Lord Jesus Christ; even as the prophets from earliest times spoke of him, and our Lord Jesus Christ himself taught us, and the creed of the fathers has handed down to us.[2]

[2] "Statement of the Council of Chalcedon," in Henry Bettenson, ed., *Documents of the Christian Church*, 2nd ed. (London: Oxford Univ. Press, 1967), 51–52. See also John Leith, ed., *Creeds of the Churches* (Atlanta: 1973), 35–36. For a comprehensive discussion of the period of the council, see Jaroslav Pelikan, *The Emergence of the Catholic Tradition* (Chicago: Univ. of Chicago Press, 1971), 226–77; R. V. Sellers, *The Council of Chalcedon: A Historical and Doctrinal Survey* (London: SPCK, 1961); John Meyendorff, *Christ in Eastern Christian Thought* (Washington: Corpus Publications, 1969); Karekin Sarkesian, *The Council of Chalcedon and the Armenian Church* (London: SPCK, 1965); Aziz S. Atiya, *History of Eastern Christianity* (Notre Dame: Univ. of Notre Dame Press, 1968).

The statement of Chalcedon sought to express the essential positive elements both from the moderate Alexandrian tradition and from the moderate Antiochian tradition. It also reflected the language of the agreement of 433 between St. Cyril of Alexandria and Patriarch John of Antioch as well as a statement from Rome known as the Tome of Pope Leo. In so doing, the conciliar statement sought to express agreement on the use of the key terms such as nature (*physis*), substance (*hypostasis*), and person (*prosopon*), which had been used in different ways by earlier teachers.

In the wake of the council, the difficult process of receiving the statement began in the regional churches. Although the Church of Rome accepted the statement, it did not immediately accept the canons of the council. The situation was even more difficult in eastern portions of the Church. By the middle of the sixth century, the patriarchates of Alexandria and Antioch were divided between Chalcedonians and Non-Chalcedonians. The Church of Armenia, strongly opposed to Nestorianism, rejected Chalcedon in 508. For a time, the Church of Georgia also rejected Chalcedon. During the reign of Emperor Zeno, the statement of Chalcedon was even rejected by many within the Church of Constantinople, especially between the years 482–518. It was truly a complicated period.

At the theological level, those who rejected the statement of Chalcedon presented a number of reasons that continued to reflect differences in emphasis in Christology and its expression.

First, some opponents of the statement of Chalcedon felt that the use of the terminology of "two natures" went in the direction of the teaching of Nestorius and his followers. They questioned whether there was a genuine contact between the divine and the human in Christ. The council had in fact anathematized Nestorius. However, the on-going teachings of extreme Antiochian theologians could not be prevented by the council. There were, therefore, continuing conflicts with regional churches that adhered to Nestorian views in areas near the Persian Empire. The Church of Armenia was especially troubled by these encounters.

Second, many opponents of the Chalcedonian statement claimed that the "two natures" terminology was a betrayal of St. Cyril's usual affirmation of "one nature of the incarnate Word." St. Cyril frequently used this terminology. In doing so, however, he was using the term nature (*physis*) in the way the council used the term person (*prosopon* and *hypostasis*).

It should also be remembered that St. Cyril recognized the use of the "two natures" terminology as understood properly in the agreement of 433. However, some of the followers of St. Cyril overlooked this fact. They continued to prefer to speak of the "one nature" of Christ when referring to the reality of his person. They can be considered "linguistic Monophysites." For them, nature (*physis*) meant person.

Third, many Alexandrians were also troubled by the fact that Patriarch Dioscorus had been deposed at Chalcedon. Although Dioscorus was not accused of heresy, many felt his deposition was unjust. Moreover, many Alexandrians were disturbed by the fact that the Tome of Leo received so much attention at the council. Some Alexandrians felt that its terminology could support the Nestorian perspectives that the council condemned.

Fourth, some of the staunch opponents of Chalcedon, especially in Egypt, continued to express the extreme Alexandrian position espoused in the past by Eutyches. They refused to acknowledge the fact that the full humanity of Christ was maintained in its contact with the divine nature. Like Eutyches, they were true "doctrinal Monophysites" because they taught that the humanity of Christ was subsumed by his divinity. In defending their position, they also strongly accused the council of teaching a form of Nestorianism.

Finally, the gradual divisions between those regional churches that accepted Chalcedon and those that did not also reflected other significant factors. Chief among these were political and cultural differences between those within the Roman–Byzantine world and those living on its boundaries and beyond. During the period following Chalcedon, those who rejected the council's teaching made up a significant portion of the Orthodox Christians living especially in the southern and eastern portions of the empire and beyond. Their opposition to Chalcedon was intensified because of persecution by some leaders of the Byzantine Empire.

The Period after the Council of Chalcedon

With a desire to heal the growing division, councils of bishops were held in Constantinople in 553 and 680. They accepted the Council of Chalcedon and addressed ongoing questions related to the description of the person of Christ. Both councils were clearly concerned with healing the widening schism. The council of 553 especially sought to clarify the statement of Chalcedon with the hope of reconciling those who had rejected it. In fact, the council anathematized those who did not accept the Twelve Chapters of St. Cyril of Alexandria. These councils eventually were recognized as the fifth and sixth ecumenical councils by the Orthodox churches of the Byzantine–Roman world. The family of Oriental Orthodox churches eventually did not formally recognize these councils as ecumenical, although it is worth noting that bishops from the Church of Armenia participated in these councils, indicating that the lines of division had not entirely hardened.

Major attempts at reconciling the two families of churches were suspended by the seventh century. At that time, the rapid rise of Islam led to new and difficult challenges for the churches. The ancient centers of Christianity in North Africa and the Middle East came under the political control of Islam by the eighth century. The political situation created a further wedge between those churches that accepted Chalcedon and the subsequent councils, and those that did not. Despite many efforts, this prevented an enduring reconciliation between Chalcedonian and Non-Chalcedonians. From that time, the two families of Orthodox churches generally went their own ways.

There were, however, some noteworthy contacts and movements towards reconciliation during the Middle Ages. Patriarch Photius of Constantinople, whose mother was of Armenian background, wrote to the Armenian Catholicos Zacharia in the ninth century in an effort to heal the division. Similar contacts, especially in the tenth and twelfth centuries, took place between representatives of the Church of Constantinople and the Church of Armenia. These theological dialogues nearly led to a formal reconciliation at the time.

Yet as time went on, opportunities for genuine encounters and theological dialogue diminished. Indeed, as the divisions became more solidified, a polemical spirit frequently characterized the relationship between the two families of churches. The churches which accepted the Chalcedonian statement were accused of being "diophysites" or Nestorians by the Non-Chalcedonians. The Chalcedonian churches rejected these accusations, since they repudiated the Nestorian heresy. Likewise, those that accepted the decision of Chalcedon accused those churches that rejected the Chalcedonian statement of being "Monophysites." The Non-Chalcedonian churches rejected these accusations because they repudiated the heresy of doctrinal Monophysitism as expressed by Eutyches. Both families of Orthodox churches, however, honored St. Cyril of Alexandria and affirmed his christological teachings.

The rapid and extensive growth of Islam after the eighth century tended to prevent further dialogue, especially between the Chalcedonian Orthodox of the Roman–Byzantine world and those Non-Chalcedonian Orthodox living in Egypt and the Middle East. Christians living in lands dominated by Islamic political power had little opportunity for theological reflection and dialogue.

Moreover, the growing alienation between the Church of Rome and the Church of Constantinople came to occupy the attention of Byzantine theologians from the ninth century to the fall of Constantinople in 1453. After the fall of the empire to the Ottoman Turks, the Byzantines also had limited opportunities for theological reflection and dialogue. Increasingly, survival in a hostile political environment became the principal concern.

Clearly, these facts demonstrate that the period after Chalcedon was a complex one involving legitimate doctrinal concerns, theological perspectives, and terminological differences.

Moreover, this complexity was also compounded by political factors, most especially the desire of many Byzantine emperors to reconcile with the Non-Chalcedonians and, thereby, avoid divisions within the empire. Some of these attempts, such as those by Emperor Zeno with his Henotikon in 482, proved to be shortsighted. Other attempts, such as those guided by Emperor Justinian between 531 and 536, nearly healed the division. Although Emperor Heraclius initially followed a policy of reconciliation in 610, he eventually turned to a policy of military conquest.

Likewise, the alienation was gradual, taking place over the course of decades, if not centuries. The differences in theological emphasis and terminology existed prior to the Council of Chalcedon. Yet Chalcedon marked the formal beginning of a division that endures to this day. This division did not occur overnight. It was a gradual process that varied in intensity from place to place. At times, there was dialogue and a restoration of communion. As time went on, however, the theological division, compounded by politics and geography, became more pronounced.

Renewed Contacts and Dialogues

New opportunities for contact between the theologians of both families of churches accompanied their involvement in ecumenical gatherings from the early decades of the twentieth century. The meetings of the Faith and Order Commission of the World Council of Churches frequently provided valuable opportunities for theologians of the Orthodox and Oriental Orthodox churches to meet and discuss common concerns. With these meetings and discussions, the centuries of formal estrangement began to be overcome.

On the 1500th anniversary of the Council of Chalcedon in

1951, Patriarch Athenagoras and the Synod of the Patriarchate of Constantinople formally called for the establishment of a process of dialogue that would lead to the healing of the schism. In this encyclical, the patriarch referred to the historic observation of St. John of Damascus, who claimed that those who did not accept the terminology of Chalcedon were "nevertheless Orthodox in all things."[3]

At the Pan-Orthodox Conference in Rhodes in 1961, the Orthodox Church formally recognized that its relationship with the Oriental Orthodox churches was one of the most urgent matters awaiting serious attention. Likewise, the patriarchs of the Oriental Orthodox churches proposed the establishment of a theological dialogue with the Orthodox Church in 1965.

During this period, highly respected theologians held a number of significant but informal theological dialogues with both families of churches. These were held in Aarhus, Denmark, in 1964; Bristol, England, in 1967; Geneva, Switzerland, in 1970; and in Addis Ababa, Ethiopia, in 1971. Each of these consultations undertook intensive theological studies of the issues related to the division. Each meeting produced a significant statement. Because of these discussions, the theologians affirmed a common christological teaching. They affirmed that both families of churches profess the historic Orthodox faith. Their conclusions also provided a valuable basis for establishing more formal theological dialogue.[4]

The statement issued at the meeting in Aarhus in 1964 provided a significant foundation for all subsequent discussions. A valuable portion of the statement says:

[3] *Orthodoxia* 26 (1951), 484–89. See also St. John of Damascus, *The Fount of Knowledge*, 2.53 (PG 94.741).

[4] See the texts in *Greek Orthodox Theological Review* 10:2 (1964–65), 14–15; 13:2 (1967), 133–36; 16:1–2 (1971), 3–8, 210–13. See also Paulos Gregorius, William Lazareth, and Nikos Nissiotis, *Does Chalcedon Unite or Divide? Towards Convergence in Orthodox Christology* (Geneva: World Council of Churches, 1981); Tiran Nersoyian and Paul Fries, eds., *Christ in East and West* (Macon, GA: 1987).

On the essence of Christological dogma, we found ourselves in full agreement. Through the different terminologies used by each side, we saw the same truth expressed. Since we agree in rejecting without reservation the teaching of Eutyches as well as Nestorius, the acceptance or non-acceptance of the Council of Chalcedon does not entail the acceptance of either heresy. Both sides found themselves fundamentally following the Christological teachings of the one undivided Church as expressed by Saint Cyril (of Alexandria). (par. 4)

Following the Fourth Preconciliar Conference in 1968, the Orthodox Church established a Preliminary Commission for dialogue. The Oriental Orthodox churches agreed in 1972 to establish a similar commission. Representatives from both commissions met in 1972 and 1978 to discuss the direction of the dialogue. These meetings laid the groundwork for the establishment of the Joint Commission for the Theological Dialogue between the Orthodox Church and the Oriental Orthodox Churches. Following an inaugural meeting in Chambésy, Geneva, Switzerland, in 1985, the full commission met June 20–24, 1989, at the Anba Bishoy Monastery in Wadi-El-Natroum, Egypt, and produced its first statement. The second statement was produced at the meeting of the full commission held at the center of the ecumenical patriarchate in Chambésy on September 23–28, 1990. The third meeting of the full commission was also held in Chambésy on November 1–7, 1993. This meeting produced a communiqué that dealt especially with the lifting of anathemas by both families of churches. In addition to these meetings of the full commission, there have been numerous meetings of subcommittees of the Joint Commission.

From its beginning, the Joint Commission has been composed of distinguished bishops and theologians who are the designated representatives of the Orthodox churches and the Oriental Orthodox churches. Many representatives have been engaged in discussions on this topic dating back to at least 1964. Metropolitan Damaskinos of Switzerland (Ecumenical Patriarchate) and Metropolitan Bishoy of Damietta (Coptic Orthodox Church) have served as the co-presidents of the Joint Commission during most of the history of the Joint Commission.

The meetings of the Joint Commission and its subcommittees have been complemented and supported by the numerous exchanges of visits by patriarchs and bishops of the two families of churches. This isolation, which once characterized the relationship between the two families of churches, has been dramatically overcome, especially in the past fifty years. In their meetings, the members of the two families of churches have engaged in prayer for unity and in discussions of theological themes.

THEOLOGICAL AFFIRMATIONS OF THE JOINT COMMISSION

The formal statements of the Joint Commission are relatively brief. Yet this brevity does not conceal the fact that the statements represent a precise and cogent affirmation of the common faith shared by both the Orthodox and the Oriental Orthodox. Since the statements come from a Joint Commission formally established by the Orthodox and Oriental Orthodox churches, they deserve great attention. They contain a number of significant points whose importance cannot be underestimated.

The statements reflect both the common doctrinal convictions expressed at the earlier consultations as well as the historical and theological study of the Council of Chalcedon and other events associated with it.

1. The Apostolic Faith

Most importantly, the statements solemnly affirm that both families of churches share the same faith. This conviction is expressed in the opening words of the Anba Bishoy Statement (1989):

> We have inherited from our Fathers in Christ the one apostolic faith and tradition, though as Churches we have been separated from each other for centuries. As two families of Orthodox Churches long out of com-

munion with each other we now pray and trust in God
to restore that communion on the basis of the common
apostolic faith of the undivided Church of the first centuries which we confess in our common creed....

Throughout our discussions we have found our common ground in the formula of our common father, St.
Cyril of Alexandria—*mia physis* (*hypostasis*) *tou Theou
Logou sesarkomene*—and his dictum that "it is sufficient
for the confession of our true and irreproachable faith
to say and to confess that the Holy Virgin is Theotokos."
(par. 1–2)

This affirmation is further strengthened in the Chambésy
Statement of 1990. The Joint Commission restates that both
families of churches reject both the Eutychian and Nestorian
heresies. In opposition to the former, both families of churches
affirm that the Logos, "the Second Person of the Holy Trinity,
only begotten of the Father before the ages and consubstantial
with Him, was incarnate and was born of the Virgin Mary
Theotokos, fully consubstantial with us, perfect man with soul,
body and mind" (par. 1).

In opposition to the Nestorian heresy, the commission affirms that both families of churches "agree that it is not sufficient merely to say that Christ is consubstantial both with
His Father and with us, by nature God and by nature man;
it is necessary to affirm also that the Logos, who is by nature
God, became by nature man, by His incarnation in the fullness
of time" (par. 2).

It is significant that the statements clearly affirm that both
families of churches reject both the Nestorian and the Eutychian
heresies. In the centuries following Chalcedon, those who accepted the decision of the council were frequently accused by
their opponents of harboring Nestorian tendencies. Likewise,
those who rejected Chalcedon were often accused by their opponents of harboring Eutychian tendencies. Indeed, they were
frequently labeled Monophysites despite the fact that they
explicitly repudiated the position of Eutyches. These unfortu-

nate and inaccurate perceptions were frequently the basis of the anathemas that were exchanged in the period following Chalcedon.

Moreover, the agreed-upon statements affirm that both families of churches share a common understanding of the hypostatic union of the divinity and humanity in the unique theandric person of Jesus Christ. The Anba Bishoy Statement (1989) says that this is a "real union of the divine with the human, with all the properties and functions of the uncreated divine nature, including natural will and energy, inseparably and unconfusedly united with the created human nature with all its properties and functions, including natural will and natural energy." (par. 8). The Chambésy Statement (1990) says that "the hypostasis of the Logos became composite [*synthetos*] by uniting to His divine uncreated nature with its natural will and energy, which He has in common with the Father and the Holy Spirit, [the] created human nature, which He assumed at the Incarnation and made His own, with its natural will and energy" (par. 3).

The statements clearly affirm that both families of churches reject not only the Monophysite heresy as expounded by Eutyches but also the Monothelite heresy, which denied that Christ possessed both a divine will and a human will.

2. Common Terminology

While they do not deal directly with the Council of Chalcedon, the statements recognize that some of the important terminology used at that council is shared by both traditions. The Anba Bishoy Statement (1989) says, "The four adverbs used to qualify the mystery of the hypostatic union belong to our common tradition—without co-mingling (or confusion) (*asyngchytos*), without change (*atreptos*), without separation (*achoristos*) and without division (*adiairetos*)" (par. 10).

The Chambésy Statement (1999) is even more explicit in affirming that both families of churches "agree that the natures with their proper energies and wills are united hypostatically and naturally without confusion, without change, without division and without separation, and that they are distinguished in thought alone" (par. 4).

While no direct reference is made to the statement of the Council of Chalcedon, it is noteworthy that the theologians felt comfortable in citing terms that are so central to the dogmatic affirmation of that council. In this way, the theologians indicate that both families of churches profess the same understanding of the relationship of the human and divine natures in Christ.

3. Different Historical Formulas

The statements recognize that the authentic faith of the Church can be expressed in different formulas which, when properly understood, are not necessarily incorrect or contradictory. As has been noted, the justification of the division between the Orthodox and Oriental Orthodox churches often pointed to different uses of the same terms to describe the reality of Christ. The Anba Bishoy Statement (1989) says:

> Those among us who speak of two natures in Christ do not thereby deny their inseparable, indivisible union; those among us who speak of one united divine-human nature in Christ do not thereby deny the continuing dynamic presence in Christ of the divine and the human, without change, without confusion. (par. 10)

Likewise, the Chambésy Statement (1990) affirms that both families of churches can continue to use the christological terminology to which they are accustomed.

> The Orthodox agree that the Oriental Orthodox will continue to maintain their traditional Cyrillian terminology of "One nature of the Incarnate Logos" [*mia physis tou Theou Logou sesarkomene*], since they acknowledge the double consubstantiality of the Logos which Eutyches denied. The Orthodox also use this terminology. The Oriental Orthodox agree that the Orthodox are justified in their use of the two-natures formula, since they acknowledge that the distinction is "in thought alone"

[*te theoria mone*]. Cyril interpreted correctly this use in his letter to John of Antioch and his letter to Acacius of Melitene (PG 77, 184–201) to Eulogius (PG 77, 224–228) and to Succensus (PG 77, 228–245). (par. 7)

The statements of the Joint Commission recognize that the same Orthodox faith can be expressed in an appropriate manner by different theological terms. Indeed, some would say that the alienation that came in the wake of the Council of Chalcedon was based in good measure upon the inability of theologians at that time to recognize this crucial perspective. In an effort to affirm the authentic faith, both families of churches held fast to their own theological formulations and rejected those of the other. Each side claimed to follow the christological teachings of St. Cyril of Alexandria. However, the spirit of charity, mutual respect and openness to legitimate theological diversity were in short supply. Sadly, the example of Cyril of Alexandria and John of Antioch, who agreed to the historic reunion agreement of 433, was neglected in the polemical period that followed.

4. The Faith Expressed in the Ecumenical Councils

The statements of the Joint Commission deal with the issue of the ecumenical councils. Both families of churches accept fully the councils of Nicaea in 325, of Constantinople in 381, and of Ephesus in 431. However, the councils of Chalcedon in 451, Constantinople in 553 and 680, and Nicaea in 787 are formally recognized only by the Orthodox churches. These four councils are not formally recognized by the Oriental Orthodox churches.

The Joint Commission has wisely sought to deal with the doctrinal affirmations expressed at these councils rather than the more formal issue of the acceptance or rejection of particular councils. The statements affirm that the two families of churches are in full agreement in their understanding of the historic Orthodox faith. This means that the Oriental Orthodox churches recognize the faith of the church as expressed in the doctrinal decisions of the councils of 451, 553, 680, and 787, although they may not formally recognize these councils as being ecumenical.

Conversely, it also means that the Orthodox recognize that the Oriental Orthodox churches profess the same historic Orthodox faith, although the latter do not formally recognize certain councils as ecumenical. The Joint Statements seek to make a clear distinction between the faith expressed at a council and the council itself. The Anba Bishoy Statement (1989) says:

> Our mutual agreement is not limited to Christology, but encompasses the whole faith of the one undivided Church of the early centuries. We are agreed also in our understanding of the Person and Work of God the Holy Spirit, who proceeds from the Father alone, and is always adored with the Father and the Son. (par. 11)

The Chambésy Statement also refers especially to the understanding of icons:

> In relation to the teaching of the seventh Ecumenical Council of the Orthodox Church, the Oriental Orthodox agree that the theology and practice of the veneration of icons taught by that Council are in basic agreement with the teaching and practice of the Oriental Orthodox from ancient times, long before the convening of the Council, and that we have no disagreement in this regard. (par. 8)

The statements of the Joint Commission point to a deeper understanding of councils in the life of the Church. The faith of the Church was full and complete in the period before the great councils. The councils did not invent the faith of the Church at a given time in history. Rather, the councils bear witness to the faith of the Church, especially in response to specific challenges. Generally in opposition to a particular distortion, the dogmatic affirmations of the ecumenical councils bear witness to the faith at particular times in history and using particular theological terms. The councils are councils of the Church. It is the Church that convenes them and interprets them. It is the faith of the Church that is expressed in and through the councils.

This perspective on the nature of an ecumenical council and its doctrinal affirmations is quite important. It reminds us that the emphasis must be placed on the faith expressed by the councils and not necessarily on the exact number of councils or the specific representatives who participated in a particular council. Indeed, even the terminology used at a particular council must be understood both historically and contextually.

The Church's reception of a particular council does not depend on the number of bishops who attend or their geographical distribution or the person who convened it. It does not even depend on whether a council was designated as ecumenical at the time of its convocation. Indeed, there have been such councils, which have been subsequently repudiated by the Church. Rather, the issue of reception is rooted in the reality of the authentic faith of the Church. The doctrinal affirmation of a council is honored and received by the Church if it bears witness to the authentic faith of the Church.

5. *The Lifting of Anathemas*

The statements of the Joint Commission recommend that the churches lift the anathemas and condemnations of the past as an important recognition of the common faith of the two families of churches and as a step towards reconciliation and unity.

The Chambésy Statement (1990) says:

> Both families agree that all the anathemas and condemnations of the past which now divide us should be lifted by the Churches in order that the last obstacle to the full unity and communion of our two families can be removed by the grace and power of God. Both families agree that the lifting of anathemas and condemnations will be consummated on the basis that the Councils and the fathers previously anathematised or condemned are not heretical. (par. 10)

During the decades following the Council of Chalcedon, some churches in both families imposed anathemas (excommunications) upon teachers from the other tradition. These anathemas reflected the growing divisions and conflicts that could be found in specific places, such as in the churches of Alexandria and Antioch, where rival patriarchs and bishops existed. These anathemas also reflected the inability of each tradition to recognize the fullness of the faith expressed in teachings of the leaders of the other.

Clearly, the theological discussions of the fifth and sixth centuries were difficult and complex. Moreover, they were compounded by cultural and political factors of the time. Because of this, some Oriental Orthodox placed anathemas upon those who accepted Chalcedon and specifically upon Pope Leo of Rome and Patriarch Flavian of Constantinople. This was done because some Oriental Orthodox felt that the Chalcedonian statement repudiated the position of St. Cyril and tended toward Nestorianism. Likewise, the Orthodox placed anathemas upon Philoxenos of Mabbugh and Severus of Antioch chiefly because they refused to accept the terminology of Chalcedon.

As a result of intensive studies of the period after Chalcedon, these teachers can be seen in a more accurate perspective. Each teacher was a proponent of a particular christological perspective and terminology reflecting issues associated with either the acceptance or rejection of the Council of Chalcedon. Given the fact that both the Orthodox and Oriental Orthodox recognize that both families of churches have maintained the apostolic faith, they can now also recognize that these teachers bore witness to the faith, although they may have reflected different theological traditions and preferred different terminology in their explication of Christology.

The Chambésy Communiqué (1993) says:

> In the light of our Agreed Statement on Christology at St. Bishoy Monastery in 1989, and of our Second Agreed Statement at Chambésy in 1990, the representatives of both Church families agree that the lifting of anathemas and condemnations of the past can be consummated on the basis of their common acknowledgement of the fact that the Councils and Fathers previously anathema-

tized or condemned are Orthodox in their teachings. (par. 1)

In recommending the lifting of anathemas, the Joint Commission recognizes that such actions would not be unprecedented. Throughout the early centuries of the Church, there were occasions when anathemas were removed as part of the process of reconciliation. The Joint Commission (1993) recommends, therefore, that the "lifting of the anathemas should be made unanimously and simultaneously by the Heads of all the Churches of both sides, through the signing of an appropriate ecclesiastical Act, the content of which will include acknowledgements from each side that the other one is Orthodox in all respects." The lifting of the anathemas should imply "that restoration of full communion for both sides is to be immediately implemented" (par. 2).

6. *Greater Understanding and More Regular Contacts*

The Joint Commission recommends that the relationship between the two families of churches be strengthened through greater understanding and more regular contacts among all members, both clergy and laity. The Joint Commission says in the Chambésy Statement (1990) that "a period of intense preparation of our people to participate in the implementation of our recommendations and in the restoration of communion of our Churches is needed" (par. 1).

With this in mind, the Joint Commission makes a number of important practical recommendations. It proposes that there be exchanges of visits by clergy and laity of the two families of churches, exchanges of teachers and students of theology, and attendance at worship services. The commission also recommends that acts of "rebaptism" not take place and that practical agreements at the local level deal with issues related to marriages.

The commission advocates that the documents of the theological dialogue be made available and that special publications be devoted to the traditions of the various churches. Both families of churches have distinctive histories. They have their own liturgical traditions and customs, which often reach back to the period before the schism. These differences in customs and liturgical practices need not be a barrier to unity. Yet it is important that there be increased familiarity with the characteristics of the various churches.

The process of restoring unity must be done in such a way that recognizes the distinctive liturgical customs, linguistic preferences, iconographic tradition, and legitimate historical character of the various ecclesial traditions. Indeed, this diversity is usually obvious in parish settings. Unity in the apostolic faith does not mean the destruction of legitimate diversity in liturgical practices, customs, art, and languages. Ultimately, this process will affirm not only that the Church manifests the apostolic faith but also that the Church is truly catholic.

7. *Common Witness*

The Joint Commission also recommends that representatives of the two families cooperate in ecumenical meetings and in providing a united witness in society. Already in the activities of the World Council of Churches and in many local ecumenical councils, the Orthodox Church and the Oriental Orthodox churches generally work together to present a common perspective on the historic Christian faith and Christian ethics. The commission also says that the Orthodox and Oriental Orthodox can coordinate their existing activities in the areas of humanitarian and philanthropic assistance. Both families can work together to address issues such as hunger, poverty, and discrimination as well as the needs of the youth, refugees, the handicapped, and the elderly.

The Chambésy Statement (1990) says:

> We need to encourage and promote mutual co-operation as far as possible in the work of our inner mission to our people, i.e., in instructing them in the faith, and how to cope with modern dangers arising from contemporary secularism, including cults, ideologies, materialism,

AIDS, homosexuality, the permissive society, consumerism, etc. (par. 16)

We also need to find a proper way for collaborating with each other and with the other Christians in the Christian mission to the world without undermining the authority and integrity of the local Orthodox Churches. (par. 17)

Some Recent Developments

Since the historic theological statements have been produced, a number of the churches have responded formally in a positive manner to the statements of the Joint Commission. From the family of the Orthodox Church, these are the Ecumenical Patriarchate of Constantinople, the Patriarchate of Alexandria, the Patriarchate of Antioch, and the Church of Romania. From the Oriental Orthodox family, these are the Patriarchate of Alexandria, the Patriarchate of Antioch, and the Church of Malankara, India. The Church of Ethiopia and the Armenian Catholicosate of Cilicia have made a positive response to the First Agreed Statement. The other Orthodox and Oriental Orthodox churches continue to study the statements of the commission.

In addition to these formal responses, there have been two important initiatives at the regional level.

First, the Greek Orthodox Patriarchate of Antioch and the Syrian Orthodox Patriarchate of Antioch came to an agreement in 1991 on the joint participation of clergy in the sacraments. The agreement affirms that clergy from both churches can join in leading the sacraments other than the Divine Liturgy. With regard to the Divine Liturgy, the statement makes an important recommendation: "In localities where there is only one priest, from either Church, he will celebrate services for the faithful of both Churches, including the Divine Liturgy, pastoral duties and holy matrimony. He will keep an independent record for each Church and transmit that of the sister Church to its authorities" (par. 9). Additionally, the statement says, "If two priests of the two Churches happen to be in a locality where there is only one Church, they take turns in making use of its facilities" (par. 10).

This statement expresses in practical ways that both families of churches share the same faith and sacraments.

Second, the Greek Orthodox Patriarchate of Alexandria and the Coptic Orthodox Patriarchate of Alexandria reached an agreement in 2001 with regard to the sacrament of marriage and related regulations. The agreement declares that both churches recognize the sacrament of baptism in each other's church. This formal recognition reflects the fruits of the theological dialogue. Furthermore, both churches recognize the sacrament of marriage blessed in the other church. This agreement implicitly discourages "dual ceremonies" and the "repetition" of a marriage ceremony in separate parishes of the two traditions.

Future Directions

The members of the Joint Commission affirm in their historic statements that there is no doctrinal issue dividing the Orthodox and the Oriental Orthodox. The Chambésy Communiqué (1993) says:

> In light of our four unofficial consultations (1964, 1967, 1970, 1971) and our three official meetings which followed (1985, 1989, 1990), we have understood that both families have always loyally maintained the authentic Orthodox Christological doctrine and the unbroken continuity of the apostolic tradition, though they may have used Christological terms in different ways. (par. 1)

How will the unity of the two families of churches be formally proclaimed and restored?

This question does not lend itself to a simple answer. First, it should be noted that the two families of churches are not speaking about the "return" of one group or the "submission" of another. Rather, they are speaking about the "restoration of full communion" between two families of local churches that share the same apostolic faith.

Some might say that the present movement toward reconciliation is unprecedented and, therefore, there is no clear historical precedent for its formal resolution.

On the other hand, some would take note of the historic agreement of 433. With this simple statement of reconciliation, Patriarch Cyril of Alexandria and Patriarch John of Antioch agreed to end the schism and to restore communion between the two local churches. This may prove to be an important historic model.

In recent years, two scenarios have been proposed regarding the formal process of reconciliation. One approach emphasizes a regional form of restoration of full communion between churches from the two families that are in close contact. This is a "bilateral" approach. The agreement already reached between the two patriarchates of Antioch and the two patriarchates of Alexandria are a step in this direction.

The other perspective emphasizes a more multilateral approach, which would involve at once all the members of the two families of churches. Some theologians have suggested that a council would have to be convened formally to proclaim the reconciliation between the two families. This council would bring together the official representatives of the Orthodox churches and the Oriental Orthodox churches. These representatives would solemnly affirm the end of the schism and the restoration of full communion in the apostolic faith. In conjunction with this council, the delegates would then join in the celebration of the Holy Eucharist. This celebration would indeed be the solemn and public affirmation of full unity.

Both families of churches will need to examine the manner in which the reconciliation will be manifested in the actual organization of the Church in specific places. The process of reconciliation and the restoration of full communion will require pastoral sensitivity, creativity, charity, and patience. Where there are currently "parallel episcopal jurisdictions," a process will have to be devised to establish one bishop in each city or region and to unite bishops into a single regional synod. This process may take some time. Indeed, the process may have to follow the reestablishment of full communion. It should be clear to all, however, that the bishop must not be seen as the symbol of disunity but rather as the sign of unity of God's people.

This means that no one should fall into the trap of believing that all organizational issues must be formally settled before the solemn reestablishment of full communion. Certainly, the leaders of both families of churches need to make an unambiguous commitment to the resolution of all organizational concerns. Yet there needs to be patience, prudence, and care that the God-given grace that moves us toward reconciliation is not held hostage to human sin. Indeed, it could be argued that the present state of disunity prevents church leaders from seeing potential resolutions. These resolutions of organizational concerns may become more evident once full unity is restored and the "scandal" of disunity is overcome.

Conclusions

The significance of the agreed statements of the Joint Commission for Theological Dialogue between the Orthodox Church and the Oriental Orthodox Churches in 1989 and 1990, together with the Communiqué of 1993, cannot be underestimated. These statements are the work of a Joint Commission composed of the official representatives of both the Orthodox churches and the Oriental Orthodox churches. The conclusions affirmed by the members come from an official body that has a very high standing.

The statements affirm that the two families of churches share the same Orthodox faith in spite of more than fifteen centuries of formal isolation and reflect the study of the "schism," a study that has been taking place, both in an unofficial and official manner, for nearly forty years. The two families of churches are now in a position to move toward the eradication of anathemas and the development of a plan to proclaim formally the restoration of full communion.

The consensus expressed in the statements affirms fundamental agreement in the understanding of the apostolic faith of the Church. Although the statements recognize that different terms have been used by the two families of churches to express this faith, there is a firm and unequivocal affirmation that the same Orthodox faith is being expressed. These statements reflect the painstaking work of theologians from both families of churches reaching back at least to 1964.

Clearly, the dialogue between Orthodox and Oriental Orthodox theologians should demonstrate to all involved in ecumenical discussions that agreement in doctrinal affirmation is of critical importance. The dialogue between the Orthodox and the Oriental Orthodox has not reflected an indifference to doctrine. On the contrary, both sides clearly desire to seek the truth of the faith and to proclaim it. Clearly, reconciliation is to be based on and expressive of a common understanding of the apostolic faith.

Now the historic conclusions of the Joint Commission must be communicated better at all levels of the churches. These statements should be studied by bishops at their synodal meetings, by clergy at their meetings, by the members of theological schools and by parish communities. The clergy and the laity need to become aware of the conclusions of the commission and to lay the groundwork for the restoration of full communion.

The God-given opportunity for reconciliation should not be lost. Many have become accustomed to this schism. Moreover, there is a danger that ignorance, pride and complacency will prevent this process of reconciliation from moving to fruition. Education is certainly needed. Even more importantly, there is also a need for a certain "change of heart." Through prayer and study, the members of the churches need to recognize the tragic consequences of Christian division. In addition, we need to recognize that division damages our witness to the world. Thus, we need to pray, as the Lord prayed, "that all may be one" (John 17:21), and we need to live our lives in accordance with this prayer.

DOCUMENTS

AGREED STATEMENT

Aarhus, Denmark
August 11–15, 1964

Ever since the second decade of our century, representatives of our Orthodox Churches, some accepting seven ecumenical councils and others accepting three, have often met in ecumenical gatherings. The desire to know each other and to restore our unity in the one Church of Christ has been growing all these years. Our meeting together in Rhodos at the Pan-Orthodox Conference of 1961 confirmed this desire.

Out of this has come about our unofficial gathering of fifteen theologians from both sides, for three days of informal conversations, in connection with the meeting of the Faith and Order Commission in Aarhus, Denmark.

We have spoken to each other in the openness of charity and with the conviction of truth. All of us have learned from each other. Our inherited misunderstandings have begun to clear up. We recognize in each other the one Orthodox faith of the Church. Fifteen centuries of alienation have not led us astray from the faith of our fathers.

In our common study of the Council of Chalcedon, the well-known phrase used by our common father in Christ, St. Cyril of Alexandria, *mia physis* (or *mia hypostasis*) *tou Theou Logou sesarkomene* (the one physis or hypostasis of God's Word Incarnate), with its implications, was at the centre of our conversations. On the essence of the Christological dogma we found ourselves in full agreement. Through the different terminologies used by each side, we saw the same truth expressed. Since we agree in rejecting without reservation the teaching of Eutyches as well as of Nestorius, the acceptance or non-acceptance of the Council of Chalcedon does not entail the acceptance of either heresy. Both sides found themselves fundamentally following the Christological teaching of the one undivided Church as expressed by St. Cyril.

The Council of Chalcedon (451), we realize, can only be understood as reaffirming the decisions of Ephesus (431), and best understood in the light of the later Council of Constantinople (553). All councils, we have recognized, have to be seen as stages in an integral development and no council or event should be studied in isolation.

The significant role of political, sociological and cultural factors in creating tension between factions in the past should be recognized and studied together. They should not, however, continue to divide us.

We see the need to move forward together. The issue at stake is of crucial importance to all Churches in the East and West alike and for the unity of the whole Church of Jesus Christ.

The Holy Spirit, who indwells the Church of Jesus Christ, will lead us together to the fullness of truth and of love. To that end we respectfully submit to our Churches the fruit of our common work of three days together. Many practical problems remain, but the same Spirit who led us together here will, we believe, continue to lead our Churches to a common solution of these.

SECOND UNOFFICIAL CONSULTATION
ORTHODOX–ORIENTAL ORTHODOX THEOLOGIANS

AGREED STATEMENT

Bristol, England
July 25–29, 1967

1.   We give thanks to God that we have been able to come together for the second time as a study group, with the blessing of the authorities of our respective Churches. In Aarhus we discovered much common ground for seeking closer ties among our Churches. In Bristol we have found several new areas of agreement. Many questions still remain to be studied and settled. But we wish to make a few common affirmations.

2.   God's infinite love for mankind, by which He has both created and saved us, is our starting point for apprehending the mystery of the union of perfect Godhead and perfect manhood in our Lord Jesus Christ. It is for our salvation that God the Word became one of us. Thus He who is consubstantial with the Father became by the Incarnation consubstantial also with us. By His infinite grace God has called us to attain to His uncreated glory. God became by nature man that man may become by grace God. The manhood of Christ thus reveals and realizes the true vocation of man. God draws us into fullness of communion with Himself in the Body of Christ, that we may be transfigured from glory to glory. It is in this soteriological perspective that we have approached the Christological question.

3.   We were reminded again of our common fathers in the universal Church—St. Ignatius and St. Irenaeus, St. Anthony and St. Athanasius, St. Basil and St. Gregory of Nyssa and St. John Chrysostom, St. Ephraim Syrus and St. Cyril of Alexandria and many others of venerable memory. Based on their teaching, we see the integral relation between Christology and soteriol-

ogy and also the close relation of both to the doctrine of God
and to the doctrine of man, to ecclesiology and to spirituality,
and to the whole liturgical life of the Church.

4.   Ever since the fifth century, we have used different for-
mulae to confess our common faith in the One Lord Jesus Christ,
perfect God and perfect man. Some of us affirm two natures,
wills and energies hypostatically united in the One Lord Jesus
Christ. Some of us affirm one united divine-human nature, will
and energy in the same Christ. But both sides speak of a union
without confusion, without change, without division, without
separation. The four adverbs belong to our common tradition.
Both affirm the dynamic permanence of the Godhead and the
manhood, with all their natural properties and faculties, in the
one Christ. Those who speak in terms of "two" do not thereby
divide or separate. Those who speak in terms of "one" do not
thereby commingle or confuse. The "without division, without
separation" of those who say "two," and the "without change,
without confusion" of those who say "one" need to be specially
underlined, in order that we may understand each other.

5.   In this spirit, we have discussed also the continuity
of doctrine in the Councils of the Church, and especially the
monenergistic and monothelete controversies of the seventh
century. All of us agree that the human will is neither absorbed
nor suppressed by the divine will in the Incarnate Logos, nor
are they contrary one to the other. The uncreated and created
natures, with the fullness of their natural properties and faculties, were united without confusion or separation, and continue
to operate in the one Christ, our Saviour. The position of those
who wish to speak of one divine-human will and energy united
without confusion or separation does not appear therefore to
be incompatible with the decision of the Council of Constantinople (680–81), which affirms two natural wills and two natural
energies in Him existing indivisibly, inconvertibly, inseparably,
inconfusedly.

6.   We have sought to formulate several questions, which
need further study before the full communion between our

Churches can be restored. But we are encouraged by the common mind we have on some fundamental issues to pursue our task of common study in the hope that despite the difficulties we have encountered, the Holy Spirit will lead us on into full agreement.

7. Our mutual contacts in the recent past have convinced us that it is a first priority for our Churches to explore with a great sense of urgency adequate steps to restore the full communion between our Churches, which has been sadly interrupted for centuries now. Our conversations at Aarhus in 1964 and at Bristol in 1967 have shown us that, in order to achieve this end by the grace of God, our Churches need to pursue certain preliminary actions.

8. The remarkable measure of agreement so far reached among the theologians on the Christological teaching of our Churches should soon lead to the formulation of a joint declaration in which we express together in the same formula our common faith in the One Lord Jesus Christ, whom we all acknowledge to be perfect God and perfect man. This formula, which will not have the status of a confession of faith or of a creed, should be drawn up by a group of theologians officially commissioned by the Churches, and submitted to the Churches for formal and authoritative approval, or for suggestions for modifications which will have to be considered by the commission before a final text is approved by the Churches.

9. In addition to proposing a formula of agreement on the basic Christological faith in relation to the nature, will and energy of our One Lord Jesus Christ, the joint theological commission will also have to examine the canonical, liturgical and jurisdictional problems involved—e.g. anathemas and liturgical deprecations by some Churches of theologians regarded by others as doctors and saints of the Church, the acceptance and nonacceptance of some Councils, and the jurisdictional assurances and agreements necessary before formal restoration of communion.

10. We submit this agreed statement to the authorities and

peoples of our Churches with great humility and deep respect. We see our task as a study group only in terms of exploring together common possibilities which will facilitate action by the Churches. Much work still needs to be done, both by us and by the Churches, in order that the unity for which our Lord prayed may become real in the life of the Churches.

THIRD UNOFFICIAL CONSULTATION
ORTHODOX–ORIENTAL ORTHODOX THEOLOGIANS

SUMMARY OF CONCLUSIONS

Geneva, Switzerland
August 16–21, 1970

The third unofficial consultation between the theologians of the Oriental Orthodox and Eastern Orthodox Churches was held from August 16–21, 1970, at the Cenacle, Geneva, in an atmosphere of openness and trust which has been built up thanks to the two previous conversations at Aarhus (1964) and Bristol (1967).

I. Reaffirmation of Christological Agreement

We have reaffirmed our agreements at Aarhus and Bristol on the substance of our common Christology. On the essence of the Christological dogma our two traditions, despite fifteen centuries of separation, still find themselves in full and deep agreement with the universal tradition of the one undivided Church. It is the teaching of the blessed Cyril on the hypostatic union of the two natures in Christ that we both affirm, though we may use differing terminology to explain this teaching. We both teach that He who is consubstantial with the Father according to Godhead became consubstantial also with us according to humanity in the Incarnation, that He who was before all ages begotten from the Father was in these last days for us and for our salvation born of the blessed Virgin Mary, and that in Him the two natures are united in the one hypostasis of the Divine Logos, without confusion, without change, without division, without separation. Jesus Christ is perfect God and perfect man, with all the properties and faculties that belong to Godhead and to humanity.

The human will and energy of Christ are neither absorbed nor suppressed by His divine will and energy, nor are the former opposed to the latter, but are united together in perfect concord without division or confusion; He who wills and acts is always the One hypostasis of the Logos Incarnate. One is Emmanuel, God and man, Our Lord and Saviour, whom we adore and worship and who yet is one of us.

We have become convinced that our agreement extends beyond Christological doctrine to embrace other aspects also of the authentic tradition, though we have not discussed all matters in detail. But through visits to each other, and through study of each other's liturgical traditions and theological and spiritual writings, we have rediscovered, with a sense of gratitude to God, our mutual agreement in the common tradition of the One Church in all important matters of liturgy and spirituality, doctrine and canonical practice, in our understanding of the Holy Trinity, of the Incarnation, of the Person and Work of the Holy Spirit, on the nature of the Church as the Communion of Saints with its ministry and Sacraments, and on the life of the world to come when our Lord and Saviour shall come in all his glory.

We pray that the Holy Spirit may continue to draw us together to find our full unity in the one Body of Christ. Our mutual agreement is not merely verbal or conceptual; it is a deep agreement that impels us to beg our Churches to consummate our union by bringing together again the two lines of tradition which have been separated from each other for historical reasons for such a long time. We work in the hope that our Lord will grant us full unity so that we can celebrate together that unity in the Common Eucharist. That is our strong desire and final goal.

II. Some Differences

Despite our agreement on the substance of the tradition, the long period of separation has brought about certain differences in the formal expression of that tradition. These differences have to do with three basic ecclesiological issues: (a) the meaning and place of certain Councils in the life of the Church, (b) the anathematization or acclamation as Saints of certain controversial teachers in the Church, and (c) the jurisdictional questions related to manifestation of the unity of the Church at local, regional and world levels.

A.   Theologians from the Eastern Orthodox Church have drawn attention to the fact that for them the Church teaches that the seven ecumenical councils which they acknowledge have an inner coherence and continuity that make them a single indivisible complex to be viewed in its entirety of dogmatic definition. Theologians from the Oriental Orthodox Church feel, however, that the authentic Christological tradition has so far been held by them on the basis of the three ecumenical councils, supplemented by the liturgical and patristic tradition of the Church. It is our hope that further study will lead to the solution of this problem by the decision of our Churches.

As for the Councils and their authority for the tradition, we all agree that the Councils should be seen as charismatic events in the life of the Church rather than as an authority over the Church; where some Councils are acknowledged as true Councils, whether as ecumenical or as local, by the Church's tradition, their authority is to be seen as coming from the Holy Spirit. Distinction is to be made not only between the doctrinal definitions and canonical legislations of a Council, but also between the true intention of the dogmatic definition of a Council and the particular terminology in which it is expressed, which latter has less authority than the intention.

B.   The reuniting of the two traditions which have their own separate continuity poses certain problems in relation to certain revered teachers of one family being condemned or anathematized by the other. It may not be necessary formally to lift these anathemas, nor for these teachers to be recognised as Saints by the condemning side. But the restoration of Communion obviously implies, among other things, that formal anathemas and condemnation of revered teachers of the other side should be discontinued as in the case of Leo, Dioscurus, Severus, and others.

C.   It is recognised that jurisdiction is not to be regarded only as an administrative matter, but that it also touches the question of ecclesiology in some aspects. The traditional pattern of territorial autonomy or autocephaly has its own pragmatic, as well as theological, justification. The manifestation of local unity in the early centuries was to have one bishop, with one college of presbyters united in one Eucharist. In more recent times pragmatic considerations, however, have made it necessary in some cases to have more than one bishop and one Eucharist in one city, but it is important that the norm required by the nature of the Church be safeguarded at least in principle and expressed in Eucharistic Communion and in local conciliar structures.

The universal tradition of the Church does not demand uniformity in all details of doctrinal formulation, forms of worship and canonical practice. But the limits of pluralistic variability need to be more clearly worked out, in the areas of the forms of worship, in terminology of expressing the faith, in spirituality, in canonical practice, in administrative or jurisdictional patterns, and in the other structural or formal expressions of tradition, including the names of teachers and Saints in the Church.

III. Towards a Statement of Reconciliation

We reaffirm the suggestion made by the Bristol consultation that one of the next steps is for the Churches of our two families to appoint an official joint commission to examine those things which have separated us in the past, to discuss our mutual agreements and disagreements and to see if the degree of agreement is adequate to justify the drafting of an explanatory statement of reconciliation, which will not have the status of a confession of faith or a dogmatic definition, but can be the basis on which our Churches can take the steps necessary for our being united in a common Eucharist.

We have given attention to some of the issues that need to be officially decided in such a statement of reconciliation. Its basic content would of course be the common Christological agreement; it should be made clear that this is not an innovation on either side, but an explanation of what has been held on both sides for centuries, as is attested by the liturgical and patristic documents. The common understanding of Christology is the fundamental basis for the life, orthodoxy and unity of the Church.

Such a statement of reconciliation could make use of the theology of St. Cyril of Alexandria as well as expressions used in the Formula of Concord of 433 between St. Cyril and John of Antioch, the terminology used in the four later Councils and in the patristic and liturgical texts on both sides. Such terminology should not be used in an ambiguous way to cover up real disagreement, but should help to make manifest the agreement that really exists.

IV. Some Practical Steps

Contacts between Churches of the two families have developed at a pace that is encouraging. Visits to each other, in some cases at the level of heads of Churches, and in others at the episcopal level or at the level of theologians, have helped to mark further progress in the growing degree of mutual trust, understanding and agreement. Theological students from the Oriental Orthodox Churches have been studying in institutions of the Eastern Orthodox Churches for some time now; special efforts should be made now to encourage more students from the Eastern Orthodox Churches to study in Oriental Orthodox institutions. There should be more exchange at the level of theological professors and Church dignitaries.

It is our hope and prayer that more official action on the part of the two families of Churches will make the continuation of this series of unofficial conversations no longer necessary. But much work still needs to be done, some of which can be initiated at an informal level.

With this in mind this third unofficial meeting of theologians from the two families constitutes:

A.   A Continuation Committee of which all the participants of the three conversations at Aarhus, Bristol and Geneva would be corresponding members, and

B.   A Special Executive Committee of this Continuation Committee consisting of the following members, and who shall have the functions detailed further below:

1.   Metropolitan Emilianos of Calabria
2.   Archpriest Vitaly Borovoy
3.   Vardapet Mesrob Krikorian
4.   Professor Nikos Nissiotis
5.   Father Paul Verghese

Functions

a.   To edit, publish and transmit to the Churches a report of this third series of conversations, through the *Greek Orthodox Theological Review*;

b.   To produce, on the basis of a common statement of which the substance is agreed upon in this meeting, a résumé of the main points of the three unofficial conversations in a form which can be discussed, studied and acted upon by the different autocephalous Churches;

c.   To publish a handbook containing statistical, historical, theological and other information regarding the various autocephalous Churches;

d.   To explore the possibility of constituting an association of theological schools, in which all the seminaries, academies and theological faculties of the various autocephalous Churches of both families can be members;

e.   To publish a periodical which will continue to provide information about the autocephalous Churches and to pursue further discussion of theological, historical and ecclesiological issues;

f.   To make available to the Churches the original sources for an informed and accurate study of the historical developments in the common theology and spirituality as well as the mutual relations of our Churches;

g.   To sponsor or encourage theological consultations on local, regional or world levels, with a view to deepening our own understanding of, and approach to, contemporary problems, especially in relation to our participation in the ecumenical movement;

h.   To explore the possibilities of and to carry out the preliminary steps for the establishment of one or more common research centres where theological and historical studies in relation to the universal orthodox tradition can be further developed;

i.   To explore the possibility of producing materials on a common basis for the instruction of our believers, including children and youth and also theological textbooks.

FOURTH UNOFFICIAL CONSULTATION
ORTHODOX–ORIENTAL ORTHODOX THEOLOGIANS

SUMMARY OF CONCLUSIONS

Addis Ababa, Ethiopia
January 22–23, 1971

The following conclusions and questions have arisen out of our informal discussions in Addis Ababa about the lifting of anathemas and the recognition of Saints:

1.   We agree that the lifting of the anathemas pronounced by one side against those regarded as Saints and teachers by the other side seems to be an indispensable step on the way to unity between our two traditions.

2.   We are also agreed that the lifting of the anathemas would be with a view to restoring Communion between our two traditions, and therefore that it presupposes essential unity in the faith between our two traditions. The official announcement by both sides that there is in fact such essential unity in faith, a basis for which is already provided by the reports of our earlier conversations at Aarhus, Bristol and Geneva, would thus appear to be essential for the lifting of anathemas.

3.   We agree further that once the anathemas against certain persons cease to be effective, there is no need to require their recognition as Saints by those who previously anathematized them. Different autocephalous Churches have differing liturgical calendars and lists of Saints. There is no need to impose uniformity in this matter. The place of these persons in the future united Church can be discussed and decided after the union.

4.   Should there be a formal declaration or ceremony in which the anathemas are lifted? Many of us felt that it is much simpler gradually to drop these anathemas in a quiet way as some churches have already begun to do. Each church should

choose the way most suited to its situation. The fact that these anathemas have been lifted can then be formally announced at the time of union.

5.   Who has the authority to lift these anathemas? We are agreed that the Church has been given authority by her Lord both to bind and to loose. The Church, which imposed the anathemas for pastoral or other reasons of that time, has also the power to lift them for the same pastoral or other reasons of our time. This is part of the stewardship or Oikonomia of the Church.

6.   Does the lifting of an anathema imposed by an ecumenical council call in question the infallibility of the Church? Are we by such actions implying that a council was essentially mistaken and therefore fallible? What are the specific limits within which the infallibility of the Church with her divine-human nature operates? We are agreed that the lifting of the anathemas is fully within the authority of the Church and does not compromise her infallibility in essential matters of the faith. There was some question as to whether only another ecumenical council could lift the anathema imposed by an ecumenical council. There was general agreement that a council is but one of the principal elements expressing the authority of the Church, and that the Church has always the authority to clarify the decisions of a council in accordance with its true intention. No decision of a council can be separated from the total tradition of the Church. Each Council brings forth or emphasizes some special aspect of the one truth, and should therefore be seen as stages on the way to a fuller articulation of the truth. The dogmatic definitions of each Council are to be understood and made more explicit in terms of subsequent conciliar decisions and definitions.

7.   The lifting of anathemas should be prepared for by careful study of the teaching of these men, the accusations leveled against them, the circumstances under which they were anathematized, and the true intention of their teaching. Such study should be sympathetic and motivated by the desire to understand and therefore to overlook minor errors. An accurate

and complete list of the persons on both sides to be so studied should also be prepared. The study should also make a survey of how anathemas have been lifted in the past. It would appear that in many instances in the past, anathemas have been lifted without any formal action beyond the mere reception of each other by the estranged parties on the basis of their common faith. Such a study would bring out the variety of ways in which anathemas were imposed and lifted.

8.   There has also to be a process of education in the churches both before and after the lifting of the anathemas, especially where anathemas and condemnations are written into the liturgical texts and hymnody of the Church. The worshipping people have to be prepared to accept the revised texts and hymns purged of the condemnations. Each Church should make use of its ecclesiastical journals and other media for the pastoral preparation of the people.

9.   Another important element of such education is the rewriting of Church history, textbooks, theological manuals and catechetical materials. Especially in Church history, there has been a temptation on both sides to interpret the sources on a partisan basis. Common study of the sources with fresh objectivity and an irenic attitude can produce common texts for use in both our families. Since this is a difficult and time-consuming project, we need not await its completion for the lifting of anathemas or even for the restoration of Communion.

10.   The editing of liturgical texts and hymns to eliminate the condemnations is but part of the task of liturgical renewal. We need also to make use of the infinite variety and richness of our liturgical traditions, so that each Church can be enriched by the heritage of others.

11.   There seems to exist some need for a deeper study of the question: "Who is a saint?" Neither the criteria for sainthood nor the processes for declaring a person as a saint are the same in the Eastern and Western traditions. A study of the distinctions between universal, national and local saints, as well as of the processes by which they came to be acknowledged as such,

could be undertaken by Church historians and theologians. The lifting of anathemas need not await the results of such a study, but may merely provide the occasion for a necessary clarification of the tradition in relation to the concept of sainthood.

12.   Perhaps we should conclude this statement with the observation that this is now the fourth of these unofficial conversations in a period of seven years. It is our hope that the work done at an informal level can soon be taken up officially by the Churches, so that the work of the Spirit in bringing us together can now find full ecclesiastical response. In that hope we submit this fourth report to the Churches.

JOINT COMMISSION OF THE THEOLOGICAL DIALOGUE
BETWEEN THE ORTHODOX CHURCH
AND THE ORIENTAL ORTHODOX CHURCHES

COMMUNIQUÉ

Orthodox Center of Ecumenical Patriarchate
Chambésy (Geneva), Switzerland
December 10–15, 1985

After two decades of unofficial theological consultations and meetings (1964–85), moved forward by the reconciling grace of the Holy Spirit, we, the representatives of the two families of the Orthodox tradition, were delegated by our Churches in their faithfulness to the Holy Trinity, and out of their concern for the unity of the Body of Jesus Christ, to take up our theological dialogue on an official level.

We thank God, the Holy Trinity, the Father, the Son and the Holy Spirit, for granting us the fraternal spirit of the love and understanding which dominated our meeting throughout.

The first part of our discussions centered on the appellation of the two families in our dialogue. Some discussion was also devoted to the four unofficial consultations of Aarhus (1964), Bristol (1967), Geneva (1970) and Addis Ababa (1971). It was thought that the studies and "agreed statements" of these unofficial consultations as well as the studies of our theologians could provide useful material for our official dialogue.

A concrete form of methodology to be followed in our dialogue was adopted by the Joint Commission. A Joint Sub-Committee of six theologians was set up, three from each side, with the mandate to prepare common texts for our future work.

For the next meetings, whose aim would be to re-discover our common grounds in Christology and ecclesiology, the following main theme and subsequent sub-themes were agreed upon:

Towards a common Christology:
a. Problems of terminology
b. Conciliar formulations
c. Historical factors
d. Interpretation of Christological dogmas today

Special thanks were expressed to the Ecumenical Patriarchate for convening this official dialogue, as well as for the services and facilities which were offered for our first meeting here in Chambésy, Geneva, at the Orthodox Center.

We hope that the faithful of our Churches will pray with us for the continuation and success of our work.

Prof. Dr. Chrysostomos Konstantinidis
Metropolitan of Myra
Ecumenical Patriarchate

Bishop Bishoy
Coptic Orthodox Church

JOINT COMMISSION OF THE THEOLOGICAL DIALOGUE
BETWEEN THE ORTHODOX CHURCH
AND THE ORIENTAL ORTHODOX CHURCHES

FIRST AGREED STATEMENT

Anba Bishoy Monastery
Wadi-El-Natroun, Egypt
June 20–24, 1989

Introduction

The second meeting of the Joint Commission of the Theological Dialogue between the Orthodox Church and the Oriental Orthodox Churches took place at the Anba Bishoy Monastery in Wadi-El-Natroun, Egypt, from June 20th to 24th, 1989.

The official representatives of the two families of the Orthodox Churches met in an atmosphere of warm cordiality and Christian brotherhood for four days at the guest house of the Patriarchal Residence at the Monastery, and experienced the gracious hospitality and kindness of the Coptic Orthodox Pope and Patriarch of Alexandria and his Church.

His Holiness Pope and Patriarch Shenouda addressed the opening session of the meeting and appealed to the participants to find a way to restore communion between the two families of Churches. The participants also travelled to Cairo to listen to the weekly address of Pope Shenouda to thousands of the faithful in the Great Cathedral of Cairo. Pope Shenouda also received the participants at his residence later.

The twenty-three participants came from thirteen countries and represented thirteen Churches. The main item for consideration was the report of the Joint Sub-Committee of six theologians on the problems of terminology and interpretation of Christological dogmas today. The meetings were co-chaired

by his Eminence Metropolitan Damaskinos of Switzerland
and His Grace Bishop Bishoy of Damiette. In his response to
Pope Shenouda, Metropolitan Damaskinos appealed to the
participants to overcome the difficulties caused by differences
of formulation. Words should serve and express the essence,
which is our common search for restoration of full communion.
"This division is an anomaly, a bleeding wound in the body of
Christ, a wound which according to His will that we humbly
serve, must be healed."

A small drafting group composed of Metropolitan Paulos
Mar Gregorios of New Delhi, Professor Vlassios Phidas, Prof.
Fr. John Romanides, Prof. Dimitroff, and Mr. Joseph Moris Fal-
tas produced a brief statement of faith based on the report of
the Joint Sub-Committee, in which the common Christological
convictions of the two sides were expressed. This statement,
after certain modifications, was adopted by the Joint Commission for transmission to our Churches, for their approval and as
an expression for our common faith, on the way to restoration
of full communion between the two families of Churches. The
statement follows:

Agreed Statement

We have inherited from our fathers in Christ the one apostolic faith and tradition, though as Churches we have been
separated from each other for centuries. As two families of
Orthodox Churches long out of communion with each other
we now pray and trust in God to restore that communion on
the basis of common apostolic faith of the undivided Church of
the first centuries which we confess in our common creed. What
follows is a simple reverent statement of what we do believe,
on our way to restore communion between our two families of
Orthodox Churches.

Throughout our discussions we have found our common
ground in the formula of our common father, St. Cyril of Alexandria—*mia physis (hypostasis) tou Theou Logou sesarkomene*—and
his dictum that "it is sufficient for the confession of our true and

irreproachable faith to say and to confess that the Holy Virgin is Theotokos" (Hom: 15, cf. Ep. 39).

Great indeed is the wonderful mystery of the Father, Son and Holy Spirit, one True God, one *ousia* in three hypostases or three *prosopa*. Blessed be the Name of the Lord our God, for ever and ever.

Great indeed is also the ineffable mystery of the Incarnation of our Lord Jesus Christ, for us and for our salvation.

The Logos, eternally consubstantial with the Father and the Holy Spirit in His Divinity, has in these last days become incarnate of the Holy Spirit and Blessed Virgin Mary Theotokos, and thus became man, consubstantial with us in His humanity but without sin. He is true God and true man at the same time, perfect in His Divinity, perfect in His humanity. Because the One she bore in her womb was at the same time fully God as well as fully human, we call her the Blessed Virgin Theotokos.

When we speak of the one composite (*synthetos*) hypostasis of our Lord Jesus Christ, we do not say that in Him a divine hypostasis and a human hypostasis came together. It is that the one eternal hypostasis of the Second Person of the Trinity has assumed our created human nature in that act uniting it with His own uncreated divine nature, to form an inseparably and unconfusedly united real divine-human being, the natures being distinguished from each other in contemplation (*theotia*) only.

The hypostasis of the Logos before the Incarnation, even with His divine nature, is of course not composite. The same hypostasis, as distinct from nature, of the Incarnate Logos is not composite either. The unique theandric person (*prosopon*) of Jesus Christ is one eternal hypostasis who has assumed human nature by the Incarnation. So we call that hypostasis composite, on account of the natures which are united to form one composite unity. It is not the case that our fathers used *physis* and *hypostasis* always interchangeably and confused the one with the other. The term hypostasis can be used to denote both the person as distinct from nature, and also the person with the nature, for a hypostasis never in fact exists without a nature.

It is the same hypostasis of the Second Person of the Trinity, eternally begotten from the Father, who in these last days became a human being and was born of the Blessed Virgin. This is the mystery of the hypostatic union we confess in humble adoration—the real union of the divine with the human, with all the properties and functions of the uncreated divine nature, including natural will and natural energy, inseparably and unconfusedly united with the created human nature with all its properties and functions, including natural will and natural energy. It is the Logos Incarnate who is the subject of all the willing and acting of Jesus Christ.

We agree in condemning the Nestorian and Eutychian heresies. We neither separate nor divide the human nature in Christ from His divine nature, nor do we think that the former was absorbed in the latter and thus ceased to exist.

The four adverbs used to qualify the mystery of the hypostatic union belong to our common tradition—without commingling (or confusion) (*asyngchytos*), without change (*atreptos*), without separation (*achoristos*) and without division (*adiairetos*). Those among us who speak of two natures in Christ do not thereby deny their inseparable, indivisible union; those among us who speak of one united divine-human nature in Christ do not thereby deny the continuing dynamic presence in Christ of the divine and the human, without change, without confusion.

Our mutual agreement is not limited to Christology, but encompasses the whole faith of the one undivided Church of the early centuries. We are agreed also in our understanding of the Person and Work of God the Holy Spirit, who proceeds from the Father alone, and is always adored with the Father and the Son.

The Joint Commission also appointed a Joint Sub-Committee for Pastoral Problems between Churches of the two families, composed of the following ten persons:

- Metropolitan Damaskinos, Co-President, ex officio
- Bishop Bishoy, Co-President, ex officio
- Prof. Vlassios Phidas, Co-Secretary, ex officio

- Bishop Mesrob Krikorian, Co-Secretary, ex officio
- Metropolitan Georges Khordr of Mt. Liban
- Metropolitan Petros of Axum
- Prof. Gosevic (Serbia)
- Prof. Dr. K. M. George (India)
- A nominee of Patriarch Ignatius Zaka Iwas of Syria
- Metropolitan Gregorios of Shoa

This Joint Sub-Committee will have its first meeting from December 5th to 9th in Anba Bishoy Monastery and will prepare a report for the next meeting of the Joint Commission.

It was also decided that the next meeting of the Joint Commission would be held in September 1990 at Chambésy, Geneva, to consider:

a. The report of the Joint Sub-Committee on Pastoral Problems

b. Conciliar formulations and anathemas. (Rev. Prof. John S. Romanides, H. E. Dr. Paulos Mar Gregorios)

c. Historical factors (Prof. Vlassios Phidas, Rev. Father Tadros Y. Malaty)

d. Interpretation of Christological dogmas today (Metropolitan Georges Khodr of Mt. Liban, Bishop Mesrob Krikorian, and Mr. Joseph Moris)

e. Future steps

It was also decide that the name of the Joint Commission would be Joint Commission of the Orthodox Church and the Oriental Orthodox Churches.

JOIN COMMISSION OF THE THEOLOGICAL DIALOGUE
BETWEEN THE ORTHODOX CHURCH
AND THE ORIENTAL ORTHODOX CHURCHES

SECOND AGREED STATEMENT

Orthodox Center of the Ecumenical Patriarchate
Chambésy, Geneva, Switzerland
September 23–28, 1990

Introduction

The third meeting of the Joint Commission of the Theological Dialogue between the Orthodox Church and the Oriental Orthodox Churches took place at the Orthodox Center of the Ecumenical Patriarchate, Chambésy, Geneva, from September 23rd to 28th, 1990.

The official representatives of the two families of the Orthodox Churches and their advisors met in an atmosphere of prayerful waiting on the Holy Spirit and warm, cordial, Christian brotherly affection. We experienced the gracious and generous hospitality of His Holiness Patriarch Dimitrios I, through His Eminence Metropolitan Damaskinos of Switzerland in the Orthodox Center of the Ecumenical Patriarchate. We were also received at two grand receptions, one at the residence of Metropolitan Damaskinos and the other at the residence of His Excellency Mr. Kerkinos, the Ambassador of Greece to the United Nations, and Mrs. Kerkinos.

The thirty-four participants (see list of participants) came from Austria, Bulgaria, Cyprus, Czechoslovakia, Egypt, Ethiopia, Finland, Greece, India, Lebanon, Poland, Switzerland, Syria, U.K., U.S.A., U.S.S.R. (Russian Church, Georgian Church and Armenian Church), and Yugoslavia. The six days of meetings were co-chaired by His Eminence Metropolitan Damaskinos of Switzerland and His Grace Metropolitan Bishoy of Damiette.

His Eminence Metropolitan Damaskinos in his inaugural address exhorted the participants to "work in a spirit of humility, brotherly love and mutual recognition" so that "the Lord of the Faith and Head of His Church" will guide us by the Holy Spirit on the speedier way towards unity and communion.

The meeting received two reports, one from its Theological Sub-Committee, which met at the Orthodox Centre, Chambésy (Sept. 20–22, 1990), and the other from its Sub-Committee on Pastoral Relations, which met at the Anba Bishoy Monastery, Egypt (Jan. 31–Feb. 4, 1990). The following papers, which had been presented to the Theological Sub-Committee, were distributed to the participants:

1.   "Dogmatic Formulations and Anathemas by Local and Ecumenical Synods within their Social Context," Rev. Prof. John S. Romanides, Church of Greece.

2.   "Anathemas and Conciliar Decisions—Two Issues to be Settled for Restoration of Communion among Oriental Orthodox and Eastern Orthodox Churches," Dr. Paulos Mar Gregorios, Metropolitan of Delhi, Orthodox Syrian Church of the East.

3.   "Historical Factors and the Council of Chalcedon," Rev. Fr. T. Y. Malaty, Coptic Orthodox Church.

4.   "Historical Factors and the Terminology of the Synod of Chalcedon (451)," Prof. Dr. Vlassios Phidas, Greek Orthodox Patriarchate of Alexandria.

5.   "Interpretation of Christological Dogmas Today," Metropolitan George Khodr, Greek Orthodox Patriarchate of Antioch."Interpretation of Christological Dogmas Today," Bishop Mesrob Krikorian, Armenian Apostolic Church of Etchmiadzin.

The six papers and the two Sub-Committee reports, along with the "Summary of Conclusions" of the Fourth Unofficial Conversation at Addis Ababa (1971) which was appended to the reports of the Theological Sub-Committee, formed the basis of our intensive and friendly discussion on the issues and actions to be taken. A drafting committee composed of

Metropolitan George Khodr, Metropolitan Paulos Mar Gregorios, Archbishop Keshishian, Archbishop Garima, Rev. Prof. John Romanides, Metropolitan Matta Mar Eustathius (Syria), Prof. Ivan Dimitrov (Bulgaria), with Prof. V. Phidas and Bishop Krikorian as co-secretaries, produced the draft for the Second Agreed Statement and Recommendations to Churches. Another drafting committee composed of Prof. Papavassiliou (Cyprus), Bishop Christoforos (Czechoslovakia), Metropolitan Paulos Mar Gregorios and Liqaselttanat Habtemariam (Ethiopia), with Fr. Dr. George Dragas as secretary, produced the draft for the Recommendations on Pastoral Issues.

The following is the text of the unanimously approved Second Agreed Statement and Recommendations.

Second Agreed Statement and Recommendations to the Churches

The first Agreed Statement on Christology adopted by the Joint Commission of the Theological Dialogue between the Orthodox and the Oriental Orthodox Churches, at our historic meeting at the Anba Bishoy Monastery, Egypt, from 20th to 24th June, 1989, forms the basis of this Second Agreed Statement on the following affirmations of our common faith and understanding, and recommendations on steps to be taken for the communion of our two families of Churches in Jesus Christ our Lord, who prayed "that they all may be one."

1. Both families agreed in condemning the Eutychian heresy. Both families confess that the Logos, the Second Person of the Holy Trinity, only begotten of the Father before the ages and consubstantial with Him, was incarnate and was born from the Virgin Mary Theotokos; fully consubstantial with us, perfect man with soul, body and mind; He was crucified, died, was buried and rose from the dead on the third day, and ascended to the Heavenly Father, where He sits on the right hand of the Father as Lord of all creation. At Pentecost, by the coming of the Holy Spirit, He manifested the Church as His Body. We look forward to His coming again in the fullness of His glory,

according to the Scriptures.

2.   Both families condemn the Nestorian heresy and the crypto-Nestorianism of Theodoret of Cyrus. They agree that it is not sufficient merely to say that Christ is consubstantial both with His Father and with us, by nature God and by nature man; it is necessary to affirm also that the Logos, who is by nature God, became by nature man, by His Incarnation in the fullness of time.

3.   Both families agree that the hypostasis of the Logos became composite by uniting to His divine uncreated nature with its natural will and energy, which He has in common with the Father and the Holy Spirit, created human nature, which He assumed at the Incarnation and made His own, with its natural will and energy.

4.   Both families agree that the natures with their proper energies and wills are united hypostatically and naturally without confusion, without change, without division and without separation, and that they are distinguished in thought alone.

5.   Both families agree that He who wills and acts is always the one hypostasis of the Logos Incarnate.

6.   Both families agree in rejecting interpretations of Councils which do not fully agree with the Horos of the Third Ecumenical Council and the letter (433) of Cyril of Alexandria to John of Antioch.

7.   The Orthodox agree that the Oriental Orthodox will continue to maintain their traditional Cyrillian terminology of "One nature of the Incarnate Logos" (*mia physis tou Theou Logou sesar bomene*), since they acknowledge the double consubstantiality of the Logos which Eutyches denied. The Orthodox also use this terminology. The Oriental Orthodox agree that the Orthodox are justified in their use of the two-natures formula, since they acknowledge that the distinction is "in thought alone" (*te theoria mone*). Cyril interpreted correctly this use in his letter to John of Antioch and his letters to Acacius of Melitene (PG 77, 184–201), and to Eulogius (PG 77, 224–228) and to Succensus (PG 77, 228–245).

8. Both families accept the first three Ecumenical Councils, which form our common heritage. In relation to the four later Councils of the Orthodox Church, the Orthodox state that for them the above points 1–7 are the teachings also of the four later Councils of the Orthodox Church, while the Oriental Orthodox consider this statement of the Orthodox as their interpretation. With this understanding, the Oriental Orthodox respond to it positively.

In relation to the teaching of the Seventh Ecumenical Council of the Orthodox Church, the Oriental Orthodox agree that the theology and practice of the veneration of icons taught by the Council are in basic agreement with the teaching and practice of the Oriental Orthodox from ancient times, long before the convening of the Council, and that we have no disagreement in this regard.

9. In the light of our Agreed Statement on Christology as well as the above common affirmations, we have now clearly understood that both families have always loyally maintained the same authentic Orthodox Christological faith, and the unbroken continuity of the apostolic tradition, though they may have used Christological terms in different ways. It is this common faith and continuous loyalty to the apostolic tradition that should be the basis of our unity and communion.

10. Both families agree that all the anathemas and condemnations of the past which now divide us should be lifted by the Churches in order that the last obstacle to the full unity and communion of our two families can be removed by the grace and power of God. Both families agree that the lifting of anathemas and condemnations will be consummated on the basis that the Councils and the fathers previously anathematised or condemned are not heretical.

We therefore recommend to our Churches the following practical steps:

A. The Orthodox should lift all anathemas and condemnations against all Oriental Orthodox Councils and fathers whom they have anathematised or condemned in the past.

B.   The Oriental Orthodox should at the same time lift all anathemas and condemnations against all Orthodox Councils and fathers whom they have anathematised or condemned in the past.

C.   The manner in which the anathemas are to be lifted should be decided by the Churches individually.

D.   Trusting in the power of the Holy Spirit, the Spirit of Truth, Unity and Love, we submit this Agreed Statement and Recommendations to our venerable Churches for their consideration and action, praying that the same Spirit will lead us to that unity for which our Lord prayed and prays.

JOINT COMMISSION OF THE THEOLOGICAL DIALOGUE
BETWEEN THE ORTHODOX CHURCH
AND THE ORIENTAL ORTHODOX CHURCHES

RECOMMENDATIONS ON PASTORAL ISSUES

Orthodox Center of the Ecumenical Patriarchate
Chambésy (Geneva), Switzerland
September 23–28, 1990

The Joint Commission of the Theological Dialogue between the Orthodox Church and the Oriental Orthodox Churches, at its meeting at the Orthodox Center of the Ecumenical Patriarchate, in Chambésy, Geneva, from September 23rd to 28th, 1990, received a report from its Joint Pastoral Sub-Committee which had met at the Anba Bishoy Monastery in Egypt from January 31st to February 4th, 1990. The report was the starting point for an extended discussion of four types of pastoral issues:

I.   Relations among our two families of Churches, and our preparation for unity

II.   Relations of our Churches with other Christian Churches and our common participation in the ecumenical movement

III.   Our common service to the world of suffering, need, injustice and conflicts

IV.   Our cooperation in the propagation of our common faith and tradition

I. Relations among our two families of Churches

1.   We feel as a Joint Theological Commission that a period of intense preparation of our people to participate in the implementation of our recommendations and in the restoration of communion of our Churches is needed. To this end we propose the following practical procedure.

2.   It is important to plan an exchange of visits by our heads of Churches and prelates, priests and lay people of each one of our two families of Churches to the other.

3.   It is important to give further encouragement to the exchange of theological professors and students among theological institutions of the two families for periods varying from one week to several years.

4.   In localities where Churches of the two families co-exist, the congregations should organize participation of one group of people—men, women, youth and children, including priests, where possible from one congregation of one family to a congregation of the other to attend in the latter's Eucharistic worship on Sundays and feast days.

5.   Publications:

    a.   We need to publish, in the various languages of our Churches, the key documents of this Joint Commission with explanatory notes, in small pamphlets to be sold at a reasonable price in all our congregations.

    b.   It will be useful also to have brief pamphlets explaining in simple terms the meaning of the Christological terminology and interpreting the variety of terminology taken by various persons and groups in the course of history in the light of our Agreed Statement on Christology.

    c.   We need a book which gives some brief account, both historical and descriptive, of all the Churches of our two families. This should also be produced in the various languages of our peoples, with pictures and photographs as much as possible.

    d.   We need to promote brief books of Church history by specialist authors giving a more positive understanding of the divergencies of the fifth, sixth and seventh centuries.

6.   Churches of both families should agree that they will not re-baptize members of each other, for recognition of the

baptism of the Churches of our two families, if they have not already done so.

7.   Churches should initiate bilateral negotiations for facilitating each other in using each other's church premises in special cases where any of them is deprived of such means.

8.   Where conflicts arise between Churches of our two families, e.g. (a) marriages consecrated in one Church annulled by a bishop of another Church; (b) marriages between members of our two families, being celebrated in one Church over against the other; (c) or children from such marriages being forced to join the one Church against the other; the Churches involved should come to bilateral agreements on the procedure to be adopted until such problems are finally solved by our union.

9.   The Churches of both families should be encouraged to look into the theological curriculum and books used in their institutions and make necessary additions and changes in them with the view to promoting better understanding of the other family of Churches. They may also profitably devise programmes for instructing the pastors and people in our congregations on the issues related to the union of the two families.

II. Relations of our Churches with other Christian Churches in the world

10.   Our common participation in the ecumenical movement and our involvement in the World Council of Churches needs better co-ordination to make it more effective and fruitful for the promotion of the faith which was once delivered to the saints in the context of the ecumenical movement. We could have a preliminary discussion of this question at the Seventh Assembly of the WCC at Canberra, Australia, in February 1991 as well as in regional and national councils of Churches and work out an appropriate scheme for more effective co-ordination of our efforts.

11.   There are crucial issues on which our two families agree fundamentally and have disagreements with the Roman Catholic and Protestant Churches. We could organize small

joint consultations on issues like:

  a. the position and role of the woman in the life of the Church and our common Orthodox response to the contemporary problem of other Christian communities concerning the ordination of women to the priesthood

  b. pastoral care for mixed marriages between Orthodox and heterodox Christians

  c. marriages between Orthodox Christians and members of other religions

  d. the Orthodox position on dissolution or annulment of marriage, divorce and separation of married couples

  e. abortion

12. A joint consultation should be held on the burning problem of proselytism, vis-à-vis religious freedom to draw the framework of an agreement with other Churches, for the procedure to be followed when an Orthodox or Oriental Orthodox person or family wants to join another (Catholic or Protestant) Church or vice versa.

13. A special joint consultation should be held on the theology and practice of Uniatism in the Roman Catholic Church, as a prelude to a discussion with the Roman Catholic Church on this subject.

14. We need to have another joint consultation to coordinate the results of the several bilateral conversations now going on or held in the past by the Churches of our two families with other Catholic and Protestant Churches.

III. Our common service to the world of suffering, need, injustice and conflicts

15. We need to think together how best we could co-ordinate our existing schemes for promoting our humanitarian and philanthropic projects in the socio-ethnic context of our peoples and of the world at large. This would entail our common approach to such problems as:

    a.   hunger and poverty
    b.   sickness and suffering
    c.   political, religious and social discriminations
    d.   refugees and victims of war
    e.   youth, drugs and unemployment
    f.   the mentally and physically handicapped
    g.   the old and the aged

IV. Our cooperation in the propagation of the Christian Faith

16.   We need to encourage and promote mutual cooperation as far as possible in the work of our inner mission to our people, i.e., in instructing them in the faith, and how to cope with modern dangers arising from contemporary secularism, including cults, ideologies, materialism, AIDS, homosexuality, the permissive society, consumerism, etc.

17.   We also need to find a proper way for collaborating with each other and with the other Christians in the Christian mission to the world without undermining the authority and integrity of the local Orthodox Churches.

JOINT COMMISSION OF THE THEOLOGICAL DIALOGUE
BETWEEN THE ORTHODOX CHURCH
AND THE ORIENTAL ORTHODOX CHURCHES

COMMUNIQUÉ

Orthodox Center of the Ecumenical Patriarchate
Chambésy, Geneva, Switzerland
November 1–6, 1993

Proposals for Lifting Anathemas

1.   In the light of our Agreed Statement on Christology at
St. Bishoy Monastery 1989, and of our Second Agreed Statement at Chambésy 1990, the representatives of both Church
families agree that the lifting of anathemas and condemnations
of the past can be consummated on the basis of their common
acknowledgement of the fact that the Councils and fathers
previously anathematized or condemned are Orthodox in
their teachings. In the light of our four unofficial consultations
(1964, 1967, 1970, 1971) and our three official meetings which
followed on (1985, 1989, 1990), we have understood that both
families have loyally maintained the authentic Orthodox Christological doctrine and the unbroken continuity of the apostolic
tradition, though they may have used Christological terms in
different ways.

2.   The lifting of the anathemas should be made unanimously and simultaneously by the Heads of all the Churches of
both sides, through the signing of an appropriate ecclesiastical
Act, the content of which will include acknowledgements from
each side that the other one is Orthodox in all respects.

3.   The lifting of the anathemas should imply:

     a.   that restoration of full communion for both sides is
        to be immediately implemented;

b.   that no past condemnation, synodical or personal, against each other is applicable anymore;

c.   that a catalogue of Diptychs of the Heads of the Churches should be agreed upon to be used liturgically.

4.   At the same time the following practical steps should be taken:

a.   The Joint Sub-Committee for Pastoral Issues should continue its very important task according to what had been agreed at the 1990 meeting of the Joint Commission.

b.   The co-chairmen of the Joint Commission should visit the Heads of the Churches with the view to offering fuller information on the outcome of the Dialogue.

c.   A Liturgical Sub-Committee should be appointed by both sides to examine the liturgical implications arising from the restoration of communion and to propose appropriate forms of concelebration.

d.   Matters relating to ecclesiastical jurisdiction should be left to be arranged by the respective authorities of the local churches according to common canonical and synodical principles.

e.   The two co-chairmen of the Joint Commission with the two Secretaries of the Dialogue should make provisions for the production of appropriate literature explaining our common understanding of the Orthodox faith which has led us to overcome the divisions of the past, and also coordinating the work of the other Sub-Committees.

STATEMENT OF THE ORTHODOX CHURCH OF ANTIOCH
ON THE THEOLOGICAL DIALOGUE
ON THE RELATIONS BETWEEN THE EASTERN
AND SYRIAN ORTHODOX CHURCHES

A SYNODAL AND PATRIARCHAL LETTER

November 1991

To All Our Children, Protected by God,
of the Holy See of Antioch

Beloved:

You must have heard of the continuous efforts for decades by our Church with the sister Syrian Orthodox Church to foster a better knowledge and understanding of both Churches, whether on the dogmatic or pastoral level. These attempts are nothing but a natural expression that the Orthodox Churches, and especially those within the Holy See of Antioch, are called to articulate the will of the Lord that all may be one, just as the Son is one with the Heavenly Father (John 10:30).

It is our duty and that of our brothers in the Syrian Orthodox Church to witness to Christ in our Eastern region where He was born, preached, suffered, was buried and rose from the dead, ascended into Heaven, and sent down His Holy and Life-Giving Spirit upon His Holy Apostles.

All the meetings, the fellowship, the oral and written declarations meant that we belong to one faith even though history had manifested our division more than the aspects of our unity.

All this has called upon our Holy Synod of Antioch to bear witness to the progress of our Church in the See of Antioch towards unity that preserves for each Church its authentic Oriental heritage whereby the one Antiochian Church benefits from its sister Church and is enriched in its traditions, literature and holy rituals.

Every endeavour and pursuit in the direction of the coming together of the two Churches is based on the conviction that this orientation is from the Holy Spirit, and it will give the Eastern Orthodox image more light and radiance that it has lacked for centuries before.

Having recognised the efforts done in the direction of unity between the two Churches, and being convinced that this direction was inspired by the Holy Spirit and projects a radiant image of Eastern Christianity overshadowed during centuries, the Holy Synod of the Church of Antioch saw the need to give a concrete expression of the close fellowship between the two Churches, the Syrian Orthodox Church and the Eastern Orthodox, for the edification of their faithful.

Thus, the following decisions were taken:

1. We affirm the total and mutual respect of the spirituality, heritage and Holy Fathers of both Churches. The integrity of both the Byzantine and Syriac liturgies is to be preserved.

2. The heritage of the Fathers in both Churches and their traditions as a whole should be integrated into Christian education curricula and theological studies. Exchanges of professors and students are to be enhanced.

3. Both Churches shall refrain from accepting any faithful from one Church into the membership of the other, irrespective of all motivations or reasons.

4. Meetings between the two Churches, at the level of their Synods, according to the will of the two Churches, will be held whenever the need arises.

5. Every Church will remain the reference and authority for its faithful, pertaining to matters of personal status (marriage, divorce, adoption, etc.).

6. If bishops of the two Churches participate at a holy baptism or funeral service, the one belonging to the Church of the baptized or deceased will preside. In case of a holy matrimony service, the bishop of the bridegroom's Church will preside.

7.   The above mentioned is not applicable to the concelebration of the Divine Liturgy.

8.   What applies to bishops equally applies to the priests of both Churches.

9.   In localities where there is only one priest, from either Church, he will celebrate services for the faithful of both Churches, including the Divine Liturgy, pastoral duties and holy matrimony. He will keep an independent record for each Church and transmit that of the sister Church to its authorities.

10.   If two priests of the two Churches happen to be in a locality where there is only one Church, they take turns in making use of its facilities.

11.   If a bishop from one Church and a priest from the sister Church happen to concelebrate a service, the first will preside even when it is the priest's parish.

12.   Ordinations into the holy orders are performed by the authorities of each Church for its own members. It would be advisable to invite the faithful of the sister Church to attend.

13.   Godfathers, godmothers (in baptism) and witnesses in holy matrimony can be chosen from the members of the sister Church.

14.   Both Churches will exchange visits and will cooperate in the various areas of social, cultural and educational work.

We ask God's help to continue strengthening our relations with the sister Church, and with other Churches, so that we all become one community under one Shepherd.

Patriarch Ignatios IV
Damascus
November 12, 1991

PASTORAL AGREEMENT
BETWEEN THE COPTIC ORTHODOX AND
GREEK ORTHODOX PATRIARCHATES OF ALEXANDRIA

2001

Since the Holy Synods of both the Coptic Orthodox Church and the Greek Orthodox Patriarchate of Alexandria and All Africa have already accepted the outcome of the official dialogue on Christology between the Orthodox Church and the Oriental Orthodox Churches, including the two official agreements: the first on Christology signed in June 1989 in Egypt and the second also on Christology and on the lifting of anathemas and restoration of full communion signed in Geneva 1990, in which it is stated that "In the light of our agreed statement on Christology..., we have now clearly understood that both families have always loyally maintained the same authentic Orthodox Christological faith, and the unbroken continuity of Apostolic tradition." It was agreed to have mutual recognition of the sacrament of Baptism, based on what St. Paul wrote, "One Lord, one faith, one baptism" (Eph 4:5).

But since up until now we are waiting for the responses of the Holy Synods of some other Churches in both families, the restoration of full communion is not yet reached between the two sides of the bilateral dialogue. And due to the pastoral consequences and implications caused by mixed Christian marriages between the members of the two Patriarchates of Alexandria, having the majority of their people living in the same countries. Those marriages being difficult to perform in both Churches at the same time or in concelebration. The result is that many sensitivities are created between the two families of the partners of such marriages. Those sensitivities which extend even after the marriage and may affect the relation between the two communities of Churches.

For those mentioned reasons, the Holy Synods of both Patriarchates have agreed to accept the sacrament of marriage which is conducted in either Church with the condition that it is conducted for two partners not belonging to the same Patriarchate of the other Church from their origin. Both the Bride and the Groom should carry a valid certificate from his/her own Patriarchate that he/she has a permit of marriage and indicating the details of his/her marriage status up to date.

Each of the two Patriarchates shall also accept to perform all of its other sacraments to that new family of Mixed Christian Marriage.

It is agreed that the Patriarchate which shall perform the marriage shall be responsible for any marriage problems that may happen concerning this certain marriage, taking into consideration the unified marriage laws signed by the heads of Churches in Egypt in the year 1999.

Each Patriarchate shall preserve its right not to give its sacraments to any persons whom she does not find fulfilling its canons according to the Apostolic Tradition.

Petros VII
Pope and Patriarch of
Alexandria and of All Africa

Shenouda III
Pope of Alexandria and
Patriarch of the See of St. Mark

Selected Observations
on the Dialogue

Ecumenical Patriarch Bartholomew of Constantinople

The work of the Joint Theological Commission has already demonstrated through common theological statements (1989 and 1990) that there is a complete agreement between us on the Christological dogma as well as the faith of the early church transmitted by the Apostles. The existing differences concerning terminology, as well as the understandable differences regarding ecclesiastical customs emerging from their long period of separation, are possible to heal since they do not touch the depth of apostolic tradition. Our experience these days of the spiritual reality of the Divine Liturgy encourages us to continue our common way towards the common cup. It is not a way without difficulties but it is offered by our Lord himself, the founder of the Church, to the apostles and their successors in the Church: "I do not pray for these only, but also for those who believe in me through their word, that they may all be one, even as you father are in me and I in you, that they also may be in us, so that the world may believe that you have sent me" (John 17:20–21).

Address to Patriarch Paul of Ethiopia
January 18, 1995
Episkepsis #515, 28.2

The official bilateral Theological Dialogue between the Eastern Orthodox and the Ancient Oriental Churches that has existed for many years now has certainly brought our two Church families closer, but this effort certainly needs our attention even more, as well as our willingness to apply the decisions that have been taken in the work of the Joint Theological Commission.

The Joint Theological Commission has been fully aware, from its very first meeting, that the "only privilege of this Dialogue" that is "absent in all the other Theological Dialogues" was and is "the fact that both Churches receive their spiritual food from the inexhaustible wealth of sources of the same ecclesiastical and patristic tradition."

The First Common Statement, despite the partial obscurities in its wording, affirmed the underlying positive prospects for a more conclusive appointment not only of the historical deprecation of the Eutychianic Monophysism by the pre-Chalcedonian Oriental Orthodox Churches, but also of the substantial agreement on the Christological issue. In this spirit and under those theological criteria that had the Christological teachings of Saint Cyril as a common basis, the Joint Theological Commission prepared and developed its Second Common Statement in the Third Conference of its plenum....

Therefore, the theological work of the Joint Theological Commission on the Christological issue and the related topics consist of a firm and trustworthy basis for the ecclesiastical approach of the utilization not only of the theological agreement, but also of the established disagreements on the relevant issues, on which the major arguments of the controversy were focused for the prospects of the restoration of the ecclesiastical communion. It is in this light and with this useful experience of the theological confrontations of an entire decade that the mission of the Joint Theological Commission has now started anew on the remaining issues to be discussed.

Nevertheless, Your Holiness, for all this to be realized we must always keep in mind that we aim only for the glory of God, and it is yet one more effort to be faithful and follow His will and desire for all of us who believe in Him to be one. He Himself taught us this: "May they all be one." It is a sacred goal that we are pursuing, and it is by our determination and unfailing interest that we will see the fruits of the grace of God multiply in our midst. It is our duty to try to see deeper than just the surface, and open our hearts and minds and pray that what had happened on the way to Emmaus will not repeat itself in our Dialogue, but we will listen with all our heart and might and with our unceasing prayer we will beseech God so that He might grant us the opportunity to once again partake together of His body and blood that He has shed for the remission of our sins and for life everlasting. For human intellect simply cannot grasp by its own devices the way of existence of the Holy Trinity and it is with this understanding that we pray that God will grant us the unification of our Churches, for this unity will come as a gift of Divine grace. Amen.

On the visit of Catholicos Karekin II of Armenia
June 21, 2006

Patriarch Ignatius Zakka I,
Syrian Orthodox Patriarch of Antioch

From our discussions so far, I come to feel that there are no insoluble problems of doctrine between us concerning the Incarnation of our Lord Jesus Christ. We (Oriental Orthodox) affirm that our Lord Jesus Christ is perfect God and perfect man, and that he is one Person and one nature. You (Orthodox) also maintain the same faith by affirming that he is "in two natures." Whereas we emphasize the union of natures, you insist on their distinctness.

Greek Orthodox Theological Review
16:1–2 (1971), 75

I would like to point out that human pride played a part in the schism regarding Chalcedon. Leo refused to accept the Second Council of Ephesus because his Tome was refuted. The Alexandrians refused to accept Chalcedon because it deposed Dioscorus and persecuted Bar Sauma. Let us not forget these human factors.

Greek Orthodox Theological Review
16:1–2 (1971), 23

Catholicos Aram of Cilicia

That trend of openness and readiness for communication continued even after the beginning of the 6th century when the Armenian Church decided not to adhere to the Council of Chalcedon where the Tome of Leo was adopted as a basic document of christological dogma, together with the formulation known as the Chalcedonian Definition. After this first shock of division in the Christian Church which began at the Council of Chalcedon and was deepened in the whole course of the 5th and 6th centuries, the Armenian Church's life and witness were not carried on in isolation from the rest of Eastern Christendom. Even in times of bitter controversies and confrontations, the relations were pursued particularly with the Greek Church, the Byzantine Patriarchate of Constantinople, with the Syriac Church tradition and with the Georgian Church.

Ecumenical Trends in the Armenian Church
www.orthodoxunity.org/articles.html

Metropolitan Bishoy of Damiette
Coptic Orthodox Church

It became a misnomer used against the followers of Pope Dioscorus that they are Monophysites. On the contrary they always confessed the continuity of existence of the two natures in the one incarnate nature of the Word of God. None of the natures ceased to exist because of the union and the term "*mia physis*" denoting the incarnate nature is completely different from the term "**Mono**physites." Perhaps the correct nomination should have been the "Cyrillian" or the "Miaphysites" instead of the "Monophysites." For example, when we say monogenis...we mean that there is **a single** and unique Son of God who is consubstantial with the Father. The Oriental Orthodox do not believe in a single nature in Jesus Christ but rather a united divine-human nature.

To conclude, our Oriental Orthodox people should realise that the Orthodox can never be Nestorians since they have condemned the Nestorian teaching of the external union of two persons in Jesus Christ and confessed that the Word of God came in His own person and that the Holy Virgin is Theotokos.

It is also clear that the Orthodox interpretation of the teachings of the four later councils of the Orthodox are the same as the doctrine of the Oriental Orthodox who have always refused both the Nestorian and Eutychian heresies. The two families are called to reinforce each other in their struggle against heresies and to fulfill their call as one body of Jesus Christ our Lord and Saviour.

The positive response of the Oriental Orthodox to the Orthodox interpretation is identified by the lifting of anathemas against Orthodox Fathers and Councils, as well as taking use of every positive element in the teaching and acts of the four later councils of the Orthodox.

The Ecumenical Movement in the Twentieth Century
www.metroplit-bishoy.org/english/Dialogue.htm

Metropolitan John Zizioulas of Pergamon
Ecumenical Patriarchate

When one reads the minutes of the discussions at Aarhus, one is struck by the growing and unreserved enthusiasm of the participants in these discussions, as they discover that many of the basic differences of Christology, traditionally known as the reasons for separation, must be attributed to misunderstandings and that the remarkable measure of agreement has been discovered....

Both Oriental and Eastern Orthodox share basically the same ecclesiology based upon the vision of the Church at the time before separation. This vision was intrinsically related to a sacramental theology expressed especially in the Eucharist. It is in the light of this kind of early ecclesiology that we have tried to approach the relations of the two churches....

Greek Orthodox Theological Review
16:1–2 (1971), 144, 160

Archbishop Tiran Nersoyian
Armenian Apostolic Church

Nationalism in the sense in which we understand it now may not have existed in the 5th and 6th centuries. Still there was exploitation and domination of class by class, of ethnic group by ethnic group. There were peoples which were different from each other and were opposed to each other. There were territorial loyalties or oppositions. Syrian, Egyptian, and Armenian social entities resisted the centralism of the Empire. These tensions, called by whatever name, played a large part in the quarrels touched off by the turn of events connected with the Council of 451.

Greek Orthodox Theological Review
10:2 (1964), 78

Metropolitan Emilianos Timiades of
Calabria (now Sylabria)
Ecumenical Patriarchate

The Aahrus meeting (1964) had a positive result for both our Churches: it led to both of us becoming aware of our nearness to each other and how few are the obstacles that genuinely separate us. It has repeatedly been said since that meeting that it was an "unofficial' one. For myself, I would wish to contest the use of this word "unofficial," for I must affirm that in my judgment it is impossible to draw a line between the official and the unofficial.

The fact that so many outstanding representatives, clergy and lay theologians, took part in the Aarhus gathering, and the wide impact that it made, are proof in my eyes of the degree to which it was instrumental in serving Divine providence. It awakened both sides from a long aged immobilism and their inertia. For the first time we began to reconsider our theological positions, and to question the outmoded formulations of our beliefs that made them appear irreconcilable. We became aware that the severe claims made by certain theologians in the past to the effect that our Churches were both ecclesiologically and Christologically separate were invalid.

Greek Orthodox Theological Review
13:2 (1968), 138

Fr. John Meyendorff

Our century has witnessed significant steps towards better understanding and doctrinal unity between Chalcedonian and non-Chalcedonian Eastern Christians. Of course, the basis identity of Christological understanding was affirmed much earlier....

In this century, the many encounters and dialogues, involving responsible bishops and theologians from both sides, have all reached the same conclusion: the Christology of St. Cyril of Alexandria is our common Christology, and the schism involves only a different understanding of formulas and expressions which have been accepted as standard and doctrinally binding by one side or the other.

St. Vladimir's Theological Quarterly
3:3 (1989), 319

Professor John Karmiris

I have read the texts on both sides of the dispute. I have come to the conclusion that there is no real difference between the Orthodox and the non-Chalcedonians as far as the essence of Christological doctrine is concerned, as all of them accept the teachings of St. Cyril of Alexandria. There is a difference only regarding the terminology and formulation of this dogma. In the same way there are secondary differences regarding worship, canon law, customs and uses, etc. But none of these should divide the Churches.

I think that when we agree about our Christological teaching, it should not be impossible to revise the anathemas. The Church is not a static entity, but a living and growing organism.

Greek Orthodox Theological Review
16:1–2 (1971), 42

Fr. Georges Florovsky

The faith of the Church as expressed in the context of a Council is interpreted by theologians. No Council ever expected it was giving the last word but only words which helped [a] wider and deeper assessment of the faith. The Christology of any one Council, for example, can not be separated from the theology of the Church. Theology and soteriology make Christology comprehensible.

Greek Orthodox Theological Review
13:2 (1968), 149–50

To understand why the non-Chalcedonians were so opposed to Chalcedon we should bear in mind the distinction between two types of diophysitism – the semantical and the soteriological. Chalcedon was wedded to semantic diophysitism. The two sides did not understand each other because there was a real lack of understanding of the soteriological Christology....The New Testament did not try to teach metaphysics but dealt with the incarnation of God to redeem mankind. The main point of Christology is to understand that manhood was redeemed through the Incarnation. The distinction between manhood and Godhead made the unity of the two soteriologically significant. That is the whole point. The formula [of Chalcedon] is an attempt to state this.

Greek Orthodox Theological Review
16:1–2 (1971), 19–20

Fr. Paul Verghese

One thing is clear. The Holy Spirit, who can always surprise us by doing what is humanly impossible, has been with us in all these conversations. And it is in His guidance and power that we continue to trust.

Greek Orthodox Theological Review
16:1–2 (1971), foreword

Recommendations for Greater Understanding and Cooperation

The Joint Commission of Eastern and Oriental Orthodox Churches

The Joint Commission for Theological Dialogue in 1990 made a number of recommendations for immediate cooperation among members of the two families of Churches. In so doing, the Commission recognized that the process of reconciliation was the task not only of bishops, priests and theologians. It was also the task of the laity. The whole People of God in each place need to be aware of the developments in the theological dialogue and to be involved in healing the schism.

The dialogue between the two families of Churches has accomplished much precisely because there is a deepened recognition that our disunity is contrary to the will and prayer of the Lord. Reconciliation certainly requires the common agreement on the Apostolic Faith. It also requires prayer for unity, mutual understanding, the healing of painful memories as well as common witness and service in Christ's name.

In all the statements issued by Unofficial Consultations and the Joint Theological Commission there has been a clear affirmation that the two families of the Orthodox Church and the Oriental Orthodox Churches share the same apostolic faith. The Statement of 1989 says: "We have inherited from our Fathers in Christ the one apostolic faith and tradition, though as Churches we have been separated from each other for centuries. As two families of Orthodox Churches long out of communion with each other, we now pray and trust in God to restore that communion on the basis of the common Apostolic Faith of the undivided Church of the first centuries which we confess in our common creed...."

Mindful of the observations made by the Joint Commission, the following practical suggestions are offered as a way of contributing to the process of cooperation, reconciliation and unity, especially here in North America. These suggestions recognize the unique relationship which now exists between the Orthodox Church and the Oriental Orthodox Churches.

Liturgy and Prayer

Members of both Churches may be encouraged on occasion to be present at the Divine Liturgy and other Sacraments in the parishes of the other tradition. This practice provides an opportunity to pray together and to appreciate the liturgical traditions of the other.

Because of the formal division between the Orthodox Church and the Oriental Orthodox Churches, there is a formal break in sacramental communion. This means, for example, that the clergy and faithful of the Orthodox Church may not normally receive Holy Communion and other Sacraments in a parish of the Oriental Orthodox. The reverse is normally also true. This is the tragic consequence of the division of the Churches. However, there have always been exceptions to this practice in times of grave pastoral necessity. Indeed, the unique relationship which exists between the Orthodox and the Oriental Orthodox provide the basis for special actions when pastorally necessary in the area of sacramental life. Already in the Patriarchates of Egypt and the Patriarchates of Antioch there are formal agreements with regard to the Sacraments.

Here in the United States, Oriental Orthodox believers, who do not have parishes of their own in a particular region, have been welcomed into Orthodox parishes. With the blessing of the local bishop and parish priest, they have been permitted to receive Holy Communion. Baptisms and Marriages have taken place. Memorial Services and funerals have also taken place. These occur with the understanding that a priest and a parish of an Oriental Orthodox Church is not available in a particular area. The Oriental Orthodox Churches have also generally followed the same practice.

Meetings of Bishops

Bishops of the two families of Churches in particular regions may seek opportunities to meet together for prayer and reflection as well as to study together issues of pastoral, theological and social concern. Regardless of the church tradition, the bishops are facing the same challenges of preaching and teaching the Orthodox faith in a pluralistic and secular society. The bishops may also recognize opportunities where they can present a united Orthodox witness and response to social and ethical questions in North America.

Opportunities may be created where all Orthodox bishops and all Oriental Orthodox bishops can meet together in retreat for prayer, reflection and study. The Standing Conference of Canonical Orthodox Bishops and the Standing Conference of Oriental Orthodox Churches may investigate the possibilities of organizing such meetings.

Clergy Associations

Likewise, clergy from the two families may seek opportunities to meet together for prayer as well as to study together issues of pastoral, theological and social concern. Parish priests in both families of Churches are facing the same pastoral challenges in this society. At the local and regional level, these clergy associations also have the potential to strengthen Orthodox fellowship and witness.

For nearly two decades, for example, clergy of the Orthodox parishes and Oriental Orthodox parishes in Rhode Island have been meeting together on a regular basis. The clergy have sponsored joint prayer services, retreats and lectures. This is a significant model which could be followed in other areas.

Spiritual Growth and Development

Under the leadership of the parish priests, parishes from both families may join together to sponsor joint prayer services, study groups and Bible studies. During certain liturgical seasons, opportunities may be found for special vesper services and lectures. Parishes and dioceses from both families of churches may jointly sponsor some special religious education programs, retreats and camp programs.

Mission and Witness

At the local level, clergy and laity from both families of Churches may sponsor activities which express a united response to the needs of the poor, the homeless and the abused in our society.

Hospitality and the Sharing of Facilities

Clergy and lay leaders may look for opportunities to invite to their parish activities the clergy and parishioners of other Orthodox and Oriental Orthodox parishes in the city or area.

Clergy and lay leaders may recognize opportunities when they are able share their church facilities with new or developing parishes of the other Orthodox family in the same city. This can include chapels for worship, classrooms for religious education, and halls.

Theological Education

Theological schools may provide opportunities for students to study the historic reasons for the division between the Orthodox and Oriental Orthodox as well as the recent statements produced by the Joint Commission. The patristic heritage, liturgical traditions, history and customs of all the Orthodox and Oriental Orthodox Churches should be studied.

For a number of decades, Oriental Orthodox students have been welcomed into the graduate degree programs both at Holy Cross Greek Orthodox School of Theology in Brookline, Massachusetts, and St. Vladimir's Orthodox Theological Seminary in Crestwood, New York. St. Nerses Armenian Orthodox Seminary in New Rochelle, New York, maintains a special relationship with St. Vladimir's.

Faculties of the theological schools may look for opportunities to sponsor symposia and lectures which examine the theological issues related to the schism and the process of reconciliation.

They may also look for opportunities to sponsor special programs of study, lectures and conferences which involve participants from both families of Churches.

Ecumenical Witness

Clergy and lay leaders of both families of Churches are often called upon to participate in ecumenical dialogue and service projects with other Christians. This is a valuable opportunity to join together and present a united Orthodox witness in ecumenical gatherings. For many decades, the representatives of both families of Orthodox Churches have provided a common and united witness in activities of the National Council of Churches and the World Council of Churches.

Conclusion

The Joint Commission of Eastern and Oriental Orthodox Churches offers these recommendations to the clergy and laity. Our prayers, mutual understanding, the healing of bitter memories, and acts of common witness must accompany the formal theological dialogue among our churches. These recommendations provide pastoral suggestions through which the clergy and laity can contribute to the process of reconciliation and the restoration of the visible unity of our churches. As St. Paul teaches us, God "who reconciled us to himself through Christ, has given us the ministry of reconciliation." (2 Cor 5:18). May our words and our deeds of reconciliation strengthen our proclamation of the Gospel in the world and glorify God, the Father, the Son, and the Holy Spirit.

The Standing Conference of Canonical Orthodox Bishops in the Americas

His Eminence Archbishop Demetrios
Greek Orthodox Archdiocese of America
10 East 79th Street
New York, NY 10021
Tel: 212-570-3500
Fax: 212-570-3592

His Beatitude Metropolitan Herman
Orthodox Church in America
PO Box 675
Syosset, NY 11791
Tel: 516-922-0550
Fax: 516-922-0954

His Eminence Metropolitan Philip
Antiochian Orthodox Christian Archdiocese of
North America
358 Mountain Road
Englewood, NJ 07631
Tel: 201-871-1355
Fax: 201 871-7954

His Eminence Metropolitan Christopher
Serbian Orthodox Church in the USA and Canada
PO Box 519
Libertyville, IL 60048
Tel: 847-367-0698
Fax: 847-367-7901

His Eminence Archbishop Nicolae
Romanian Orthodox Archdiocese in America & Canada
5410 N. Newland Avenue
Chicago, IL 60656-2026
Tel: 773-774-1677
Fax: 773-774-1805

His Eminence Metropolitan Joseph
Bulgarian Eastern Orthodox Church
550-A West 50th Street
New York, NY 10019
Tel: 212-246-4608
Fax: 212-246-4608

His Eminence Metropolitan Nicholas of Amissos
American Carpatho Russian Orthodox Diocese in the USA
312 Garfield Street
Johnstown, PA 15906
Tel: 814-539-9143
Fax: 814-536-4699

His Eminence Metropolitan Constantine of Irinoupolis
Ukrainian Orthodox Church of the USA
PO Box 495
South Bound Brook, NJ 08880
Tel: 732-356-0090
Fax: 732-356-5556

His Grace Bishop Ilia of Philomelion
Albanian Orthodox Diocese of America
6455 Silver Dawn Lane
Las Vegas, NV 89118
Tel: 702-221-8245
Fax: 702-221-9167

The Standing Conference of Oriental Orthodox Churches of America

His Eminence Archbishop Khajag Barsamian
Armenian Church in America
630 Second Avenue
New York, NY 10016-4885
Tel: 212-686-0710
Fax: 212-447-6674

His Grace Bishop David
Coptic Orthodox Church,
Archdiocese of North America
5 Woodstone Drive
Cedar Grove, NJ 07009-0373
Tel: 973-857-0078
Fax: 973- 857-1315

His Eminence Archbishop Abune Matthias
Ethiopian Orthodox Archdiocese of America
PO Box 77262
Washington, DC 20013
Tel: 301-894-2409
Fax: 301-894-0924

His Eminence Archbishop Mor Titus Yeldho
Malankara Syrian Orthodox Archdiocese of North America
611 Roosevelt Avenue
Carteret, NJ 07008
Tel: 732-969-0085

His Eminence Archbishop Mor Cyril Aphrem Karim
Syrian Orthodox Archdiocese, Eastern, US
260 Elm Avenue
Teaneck, NJ 07666
Tel: 201-801-0660
Fax: 201-801-0603